D1329582

Conditional Press
Influence in Politics

LEXINGTON STUDIES IN POLITICAL COMMUNICATION

Series Editor: Robert E. Denton Jr., Virginia Tech

This series encourages focused work examining the role and function of communication in the realm of politics including campaigns and elections, media, and political institutions.

TITLES IN SERIES:

Conditional Press Influence in Politics

Adam J. Schiffer

LEXINGTON BOOKS
A division of
ROWMAN & LITTLEFIELD PUBLISHERS, INC.
Lanham • Boulder • New York • Toronto • Plymouth, UK

LEXINGTON BOOKS

A division of Rowman & Littlefield Publishers, Inc.
A wholly owned subsidiary of The Rowman & Littlefield Publishing Group, Inc.
4501 Forbes Boulevard, Suite 200
Lanham, MD 20706

Estover Road
Plymouth PL6 7PY
United Kingdom

British Library Cataloguing in Publication Information Available

Library of Congress Cataloging-in-Publication Data

Schiffer, Adam Joseph.
  Conditional press influence in politics / Adam J. Schiffer.
    p. cm.
  Includes bibliographical references.
  ISBN-13: 978-0-7391-2209-9 (cloth : alk. paper)
  ISBN-10: 0-7391-2209-6 (cloth : alk. paper)
  1. Mass media—Political aspects—United States. 2. Press and politics—United States.
3. Journalism—Political aspects—United States. I. Title. P95.82.U6S338 2008
    320.973--dc22   2008006037

Printed in the United States of America

∞™ The paper used in this publication meets the minimum requirements of American
National Standard for Information Sciences—Permanence of Paper for Printed Library
Materials, ANSI/NISO Z39.48-1992.

Contents

Acknowledgements

I'd like to thank all of the people who aided this project with their money, guidance, time, or love, in that order. First, I am grateful to the National Science Foundation, whose grant (SES-0136850) enabled the conflicts data collection. The TCU political science department also chipped in a few bucks to help pay the coders for the Supreme Court data.

Next, I extend my most sincere thanks to my mentor, Michael MacKuen. His wisdom and patience were the right counterbalance to my youthful exuberance and occasional stubbornness. I am also grateful to Jim Stimson, Marco Steenbergen, Stuart Macdonald, and John Hardin for their substantive and statistical consultation. I also need to mention the scholars who helped me discover the joys of studying journalism, politics, or both: Susan Paterno, Fred Smoller, Ron Steiner, Mark Mattern, Kim Fridkin, Pat Kenney, and Ken Goldstein. As the last couple of years of this project were spent far out of the sphere of influence of any mentors, all errors or shortcomings are entirely my own.

I also owe a debt of gratitude to the great political communication scholar Timothy Cook. His body of work spurred my thinking at the early stages of conception and writing, and our brief conversations during my formative years provided helpful guidance as to how to navigate a subfield of political science that tends to be pushed to the fringes. The field is diminished by his untimely passing, but permanently enriched by his contributions.

I also received valuable feedback during the two University of North Carolina American Politics Research Group meetings at which I presented chapters. The rigorous, challenging APRG setting was the perfect training ground. Next, I am indebted to Andrea McAtee for the remarkable amount of time she was willing to spend reading and coding thousands of articles, and to Evan Parker-Stephen and Susan Glover for their fast and skillful coding of the conflicts data. Again, I thank the NSF for rendering my "indebtedness" to them spiritual rather than financial. I also thank Brian Fogarty for his collaboration on the collection of the economic data. I am also grateful for the assistance of Mark Horvit and Jack Douglas of the *Fort Worth Star-Telegram* and Todd Gillman of the *Dallas Morning News*.

Finally, I owe immeasurable gratitude to my father, Michael Brian Schiffer. The example he has set as a successful academic and family man showed me that this is a lifestyle worth pursuing. His encouragement and guidance at all steps in the process have been indispensable. I am also indebted to my mother Annette, whose patience and wisdom have helped me get through some tough times, and to my wife Becky, for reminding me what really matters. I also thank Alec Ewald, Greg Petrow, and Dustin Howes for continual intellectual stimulation and encouragement.

Chapter One

Introduction

"An old newsroom adage says that if both parties are angry with you, you might be doing something right." —Deborah Howell, *Washington Post* ombudsman, in her January 1, 2006, column

If there is any truth to Ms. Howell's lament, then the press is *really* doing something right these days. Both left and right are now equipped with a large infrastructure of organizations, websites, and commentators devoted to criticizing the press for being biased against their side. Though conservative critics have been at it longer—from Spiro Agnew's denunciation of the press as "nattering nabobs of negativism" to former CBS producer Bernard Goldberg's best-selling 2002 book *Bias*—the left has begun to hit back.

Nothing gets the bias cops' blood, ink, and bandwidth flowing like a controversial war. The conservative Media Research Center did not even wait until President George W. Bush declared an end to major combat operations in Iraq to issue a special report, "Grading TV's War News" (Baker and Noyes 2003), attacking the broadcast and cable media for "too little skepticism of enemy propaganda" and "too much mindless negativism about America's military prospects." Shortly thereafter, the liberal group Fairness and Accuracy In Reporting issued its own assessment, "Amplifying Officials, Squelching Dissent" (Rendall and Broughel 2003). Its content analysis of television war coverage found that "official voices have dominated U.S. network newscasts, while opponents of the war have been notably underrepresented."

These complaints about war coverage from conservatives and liberals—too negative and too reliant on official U.S. sources, respectively—are among the most common themes articulated by each side. As each group uses these alleged patterns to argue that the press is biased against its side, they appear to be irreconcilable assertions. However, if we take a step back from the ideological

1

warfare, it turns out that the patterns are not incompatible at all, but in fact are derived from the same core principles of news media behavior.

Start with a basic insight: The political press aims to live up to its professional ideals, while generating as much revenue as possible and keeping costs low. From the revenue-generation mandate comes the need to garner as large an audience as possible, which in turn leads to the well-known bias toward conflict and novelty. Conservatives can complain all they want that the "good news" in Iraq is being ignored while every death and explosion makes the front page; but to media scholars and practitioners, it sounds as naïve as asking, "Why don't they cover all the planes that *don't* crash?"

On the other side, financial pressures lead journalists to develop routines to minimize the time and resources needed for a story. One well-documented consequence is the tendency of American political news to give far more voice to highly accessible U.S. officials than to any other type of political actor. Liberals can complain about the consequences of this for the quality of war news, but they are fighting against a well-engrained norm of the profession.

This suggests that, if we are to grasp the modern relationship between press and politics, we need to understand the core norms and constraints of professional journalism. This book uses the tools of empirical political science, augmented by an understanding of press norms and routines, to tackle the following question: Under what circumstances does the press wield independent influence as a political institution? This inquiry is intended to help scholars of American political behavior and institutions weave the press into their research projects.

In short, the influence of the press comes from its ability to shape the universe of political phenomena into a discrete news product. Within a given political realm, the greater the extent to which journalists incur a financial or prestige penalty for straying from their professional norms and constraints, the more the news product is shaped in accordance with those mandates. On the other hand, the greater the degree to which a political realm contains motivated, unified elites or a readily perceivable "reality," the less leeway journalists have in warping it into an idiosyncratic news product, and thus the less independent influence they exert. These ideas are developed in a theoretical framework and illustrated in three empirical studies of news content: economic news, coverage of foreign wars, and coverage of Supreme Court decisions.

THE NEWS MEDIA AS A POLITICAL INSTITUTION

Though political scientists are far more sophisticated than the bias cops, they have their own problems with integrating press behavior into their analyses and theories. With few exceptions, treatment of the news media within the American politics subfield consists of direct measurements of the media's effect on phenomena such as public opinion, elections and electoral behavior, official discourse, and the policy agenda. The press's appearance in quantitative political behavior and process studies is limited primarily to the use of news content as an independent variable. The notion that the news media are a political institution, to be scrutinized similarly to other linkage institutions such as interest groups and parties, is not taken seriously by mainstream political science.

Recently, Cook (1998) and Sparrow (1999) made compelling book-length cases for viewing the press as a political institution (see also Schudson 2002). They each argue that traditional mainstream American news organizations, despite their well-understood across-media differences, share enough common characteristics to be viewed usefully as a singular institution (Cook, 84; Sparrow, 8–10). They then argue persuasively that the press meets all criteria for a political institution (Cook, 75–83; Sparrow, 130–37). After reviewing research showing the multitude of ways in which the press shapes and constrains the behavior and strategies of various actors in the political system — from the president "going public" (Kernell 1997) to members of Congress communicating with each other and the public through the press — Cook concludes that "there is no political institution that does not have some sort of link between publicity and governing. . . [Thus] it is increasingly tough to envision government operating without the news media's communicative abilities or political actors whose functions do not include a sizable amount of mass-mediated communication" (118–19). Likewise, Sparrow argues that "as an institution, the news media constrain the choice sets of. . . those working in the three formal branches of government, in public administration, and at various stages or parts of the political process" (10).

EFFECTS OF NEWS CONTENT: BEYOND ALL OR NOTHING

Time will tell whether this argument compels political scientists to confer linkage-institutional status to the press. In the meantime, the failure to treat the press as an institution results in a tendency for mainline behavior and institutional scholars to deal with it in one of two extreme fashions:

1) Many empirical models ignore any independent effect of press organizations or news content. For example, Cook (1998) notes that Kingdon's (1984) "otherwise superb pioneering study of agenda processes. . . neglect[s] one key actor: the media" (11). To use a newer example, the *Macro Polity* project (Erikson, MacKuen, and Stimson 2002) is a remarkable empirical

demonstration of the government's responsiveness to public opinion and the effect of policy output on subsequent public opinion. The one glaring omission, however, is recognition that the path between policy and public opinion—or the path between virtually anything and public opinion for that matter—is mediated.

2) To the other extreme, when news content serves as an independent variable, such studies often unwittingly grant more explanatory power to news organizations than is warranted. When a media effect is measured, one can say with empirical confidence that *news content* wields the observed effect. Less clear, however, is the extent to which *news organizations* themselves are responsible for the variation. Studies that treat news content as exogenous force the tacit assumption that the observed effect of variation in news content is attributable entirely to the news organizations themselves. While no credible media effects scholar would make this assumption explicitly, factors left exogenous are assumed to carry the full explanatory weight attributed to them within a model.

For the political institutions that are taken seriously within political science, one of the most consequential inquiries is into the conditions under which they wield power over each other and in the system as a whole. For example, under what conditions are parties powerful in Congress (Conditional Party Government)? Under what circumstances does Congress control the bureaucracy? When do interest groups affect policy outcomes? An important step in taking the press seriously as a political institution, therefore, is to understand when news organizations are independent actors in the political process, and when they cede their influence to other actors and phenomena.

Standing on the shoulders of those who have shown convincingly that the media matter, this book articulates a theory of why they matter, and when. This is not a direct study of the media's effect on public opinion, elections, policy outcomes, or anything else for that matter. It takes as a matter of faith—albeit a faith bolstered by years of compelling, robust media-effect findings—that news content carries a tremendous influence over many facets of American politics. The goal is not to add to the wealth of agenda setting, priming, or framing evidence. Rather, it is to understand the character, implications, and limits of such effects through an examination of the *news content* shown to wield such effects. To keep the empirical analysis relatively straightforward, and consistent across chapters, I focus on explaining variation in one particular aspect of the newsmaking process: the factors that set the press's agenda. The predictions put forth in the theory, however, also apply to other potential media effects.

The model of media influence in this book is intended to be parsimonious, testable, and easily transferable to the research projects in the mainstream study of American political behavior and institutions. The purpose is to provide a small set of propositions from which the press's role in a wide variety of political processes can be deduced. Though the simplified rendering of the news-making process may be unsatisfying to press scholars who take a richer theoretical approach, or normatively suspect to those of the critical/neo-Marxist persuasion, it is designed to condense insights from a wide variety of approaches into a relatively parsimonious set of original propositions about the degree to which the press is likely to wield influence in a given political domain. One of the key goals is to bridge a gap between subfields of American politics.

PLAN OF THE BOOK

The book proceeds as follows: Chapter 2 discusses the logic of media influence. Press effects are split into two categories, "independent"—meaning the news organization *itself* is wielding influence through its output—and "spurious"—by which the power of news content over the political process can be explained by forces that are external to the news organization. It also catalogues several of the most important norms, patterns, and routines from which the news media derive their power over other political actors and processes. Chapter 3 articulates the theory of conditional media influence. That is, in what political domains can we expect the press to wield independent influence? And under what conditions do they cede it to other actors and phenomena?

The rest of the book illustrates the conceptual framework and theory by modeling the systematic determinants of news content in three different political domains, each with differing implications for the press's role in the political process. Chapter 4 examines *New York Times* coverage of the economy. By parsing economic news into two different types—one driven by concrete external factors and the other more open to news judgment—it serves as a direct test of the theory of conditional media influence. Chapter 5 builds the first large-scale model of foreign conflicts coverage in the American press. In examining which post–Cold War civil wars received more coverage than others, it tests the press's routine-driven news judgment against the president's desire to set the foreign-news agenda. It also assesses the degree to which the actual magnitude of a conflict affects its relative coverage. Chapter 6 asks why some Supreme Court cases receive more coverage than others, using coverage from several national outlets of the 2002 Court term. To tap the crucial but difficult to measure notion of "newsworthiness," this chapter uses journalists as expert coders to build a more powerful measure of a case's fit with classic news judgment criteria. Finally, chapter 7 ties the previous chapters together and discusses the effect of the fast-changing contemporary media landscape on political behavior and processes.

Chapter Two

Understanding Media Influence in Politics

When is a media effect really a *media* effect? This chapter lays out a framework for understanding the potential influence of news organizations (as opposed to news content) in different political arenas. Specifically, a distinction is made between "independent media influence," meaning a press effect stemming solely from the unique organizational attributes of media organizations, and "spurious media influence," meaning an apparent press effect that is actually attributable to external forces such as government actors.

The most common political science treatment of the press is represented in the right-hand-side relationship in Figure 2.1, "Media Effect." Among the phenomena demonstrated to be most affected by news content are public attitudes and learning, electorate and candidate behavior, electoral outcomes, officeholder behavior, and institutional processes. In other words, almost everything in politics is mediated.

The framework, however, focuses on political news as a dependent variable (the "News-Making Process" portion of Figure 2.1). Though this question of who sets the media's agenda receives considerable attention in mass communication, it is mostly ignored, or at best given superficial treatment, by political scholars who use news content in broader analyses of behavior or institutional processes. To form a fuller understanding of the press's influence—as an independent political institution—over such behavior and processes, however, this book takes a step back in the causal chain and shines a spotlight on the determinants of variation in political news content, and what they mean for its power over the political process.

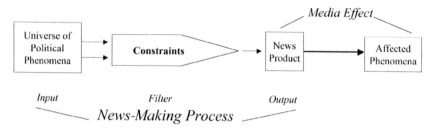

Figure 2.1.   News Content: Causes and Effects

THE NEWS-MAKING PROCESS

Let's start with a common textbook rendering of political news creation (left-hand-side of Figure 2.1). The input is the entire universe of potentially news-worthy political phenomena—every word and action from the president, every bill passed and word spoken on the Senate floor, new polls or economic numbers, politically relevant overseas events, a member of Congress storing bags of money in a freezer or soliciting sex in an airport bathroom, and so on. The output is the news product—the tiny subset of the input that makes it into a twenty-two-minute newscast, onto the news pages of a local or national newspaper, or into a cable news segment. Finally, the news organization is the filter that stands between the unwieldy universe of political reality and the discrete daily news product. The filter is the sum of all journalistic norms, routines, values, constraints, incentives, and imperatives that affect the final news product.

The filtration process is important to understanding the press's influence in politics, and deserves more careful explication in political science studies that utilize news content. I refer to all of the factors that affect this process as *norms* or *constraints* that shape the behavior of reporters, editors, and publishers/owners in their quest to assemble a product. Norms consist of the various ideas, philosophies, and values that distinguish the press from other forms of commercial media such as entertainment-oriented television shows. Constraints are the limitations imposed on organizations by the commercial nature of the American news media (public television and radio notwithstanding), as well as by the logistical challenges of a given medium.

The following typology of norms and constraints, while by no means comprehensive, encompasses many aspects of news making that are crucial to understanding the media's political role (see Sparrow 1999, Shoemaker and Reese 1996, and Bennett 2005 for exemplary, detailed treatments of these and many more. See Tuchman 1978, Epstein 1973, Sigal 1973, and Gans 1979 for sociological examinations of the news production process. And see Hamilton 2004 and Niven 2005 for economic interpretations of press constraints).

CORE NORMS OF THE NEWS PROFESSION

The press, as the only American business with a constitutional amendment granting it a virtual blank check, is constrained by a heightened responsibility to serve the public interest. This expectation has been enforced over the years by actors ranging from today's scholars, critics, and journalism schools to the founding fathers. Though the core norms that define the profession, by themselves, are not particularly predictive of news content—as they tend to be warped beyond recognition by engrained routines that flow from the financial and logistical demands of the profession—they nonetheless serve as a fitting baseline for understanding the journalistic mindset, and thus are a good starting point in analyzing the filter.

Perhaps no single source better summarizes the essence of American journalistic norms than Kovach and Rosenstiel's (K&R) (2001) book *The Elements of Journalism: What Newspeople Should Know and the Public Should Expect*. Widely adopted as a journalism text, it siphons a "description of the theory and culture of journalism" from in-depth interviews of journalists, scholarly input, and content studies (11–12). The authors boil their formidable research down to nine core principles, or "elements of journalism":

1. Journalism's first obligation is to the truth.
2. Its first loyalty is to citizens.
3. Its essence is a discipline of verification.
4. Its practitioners must maintain an independence from those they cover.
5. It must serve as an independent monitor of power.
6. It must provide forum for public criticism and compromise.
7. It must strive to make the significant interesting and relevant.
8. It must keep the news comprehensive and proportional.
9. Its practitioners must be allowed to exercise their personal conscience. (12–13.)

Taking advantage of thematic connections between the nine elements, the ideas are outlined and elaborated here in three broader categories: *truth seeking*, *watchdog*, and *democratic facilitation*.

Truth Seeking

Even as they undoubtedly know better, many journalists claim merely to be holding a mirror to society. The "mirror model"—famously articulated by Walter Cronkite in his CBS Evening News sign-off, "That's the way it is"—is a favorite target of mass communication scholars who study the ways in which organizational norms and constraints distort and pummel "reality" (the input) into an unrecognizable output. Surely the mirror analogy rests on untenable practical and epistemological grounds, as no twenty-two-minute newscast could encompass all potentially newsworthy phenomena, nor can the inherent contestation in politics be boiled down to an essential "truth." Nonetheless, it is an undeniable fact that journalists *seek* the truth. And a careful understanding of this search yields insight into the news media's role in politics.

Truth—or, more precisely, a comprehensive, faithful transmission of political reality into news content—is like a rainbow. Though it is impossible to touch, we can tell whether we are walking toward or away from it. In other words, journalistic routines can be evaluated by the extent to which they facilitate meaningful truth seeking. The use of methods designed to discover facts and test their accuracy is what K&R call "the discipline of verification" (71). They argue that "the first principle of journalism—its disinterested pursuit of truth—is ultimately what sets it apart from all other forms of communications" (42).

Watchdog

The unique role of journalists in a representative democracy, and the one that affords them constitutional protection, is to serve as an independent monitor of power, wherever that power may lie. Though K&R point to factors leading to a recent weakening of the press's effectiveness as a watchdog, such as a proliferation of "faux-watchdogism" aimed more at ratings than effective monitoring (112), they trace a clear lineage from colonial America to modern "investigative reporting" in demonstrating the primacy of the watchdog role in the American journalist's consciousness.

A mandate that flows from power monitoring is independence, not just from the government, but also from any interested faction in the political process (97). In the place of the vague notion of "neutrality," K&R note that journalists share a belief that, regardless of their personal ideology, they must maintain an "independence of spirit" (98).

Democratic Facilitation

K&R argue that news should be a forum that facilitates political discussion among all segments of society, not just the affluent or politically elite (134–35). They also argue that "journalism's first loyalty is to its citizens" (51). Reporters and editors should stay focused on serving the public rather than publishers, their families, sponsors, or special interests. They also should refrain from belittling citizens, and minimizing the democratic component of the product and its consumption, by referring to them as "customers" (60).

REALISTIC NORMS AND THEIR IMPLICATIONS

If the core norms of the profession were the most important ingredient in the news production mixture, then critics would have few qualms with political news. Unfortunately, two factors complicate the attempt to bring these norms to fruition: misapplication of them and their clash with financial constraints. The latter will be discussed in detail shortly. But first, the misapplication of the norms informs many prominent theories of news production.

"He Said/She Said" Journalism

The principles of truthfulness and independence have been warped over the years into the vague notions of "objectivity" and "neutrality" (K&R, 72). In fact, one of the loudest complaints by contemporary press critics is that pathological aversion to the charge of ideological bias has resulted in a sterile, passive press. K&R call it the "journalism of assertion" (75–79); others call it "he said/she said" or "stenographic" journalism. But the charge is the same: Instead of evaluating the veracity of the claims made in elite press-release posturing and debate—thereby moving us in the direction of the truth-seeking rainbow—reporters merely transmit the claims in equal doses. In essence, the story reads: "Democrats say it's raining; Republicans say it's not raining." But at no point does the reporter look out the window to see if it is raining.[1] In a widely distributed 2003 essay in *Columbia Journalism Review*, Managing Editor Brent Cunningham urges a "re-thinking" of objectivity, noting that the current rendering of objectivity "[makes] us passive recipients of news, rather than aggressive analyzers and explainers of it."

Official-Sources Bias

It is well documented in mass communication studies that officials tend to be favored over non-governmental actors as sources for political stories (Sigal 1973, Gans 1979, Brown, Bybee, Wearden, and Straughan 1987, Soloski 1989, Berkowitz 1987). In addition to the fact that government officials are the easiest sources to cover because they provide a steady stream of press releases and speeches, the modern rendering of objectivity plays a role. In an effort to appear objective, journalists tend to defer to sources as high in an accepted hierarchy (the government, etc.) as possible (Cook 1998). Despite its connection to perceived "objectivity," the privileging of official sources is itself a bias, in that the voices of many actors with a stake in particular political processes (especially citizens) are left out of the national dialogue.

Elite Consensus/Indexing

A related pattern is the "indexing" of the tenor of coverage to the range of debate among the most powerful governmental officials (Bennett 1990; Bennett, Lawrence, and Livingston 2007). If both sides of the dominant American partisan/ideological cleavage agree on a particular issue, then the media will cover only the bilaterally agreed upon "correct" side of the issue, refusing to enterprise opposition in the realm of consensus (Hallin 1984, Brody 1991). An implication of this is that negative coverage of an incumbent party/official can be predicted by the extent of vocal, official opposition. Also, as Hallin (1984) illustrated with the Vietnam War, the news audience must wait until an "official" critic of administration policy, such as a senator, comes forth before the press will air meaningful dissent. This results in slanted news coverage of "consensus" issues, even if there is grassroots opposition to the dominant position. A good example of this is campaign finance reform in the 1990s, prior to senators John McCain and Russ Feingold lending official legitimacy to it during the next decade. It also causes issues that might be important to a large number of citizens, but that have not entered the radar screen of national officeholders, to be left off the table completely. Drug law reform, for example—most notably decriminalization of marijuana—seldom penetrates the elite press despite a formidable grassroots structure that favors it.

Balance

One of the most common (mis)applications of objectivity is the attempt to give "both" sides of an issue or both major-party candidates coverage that is comparable in amount and tone (see Sparrow 1999, 121–23). This requires pigeonholing complex issues into two sides. It can also clash with truthfulness or proportionality if political reality slants toward one candidate or side of an issue (Kuklinski and Sigelman 1992, Niven 2002, Schiffer 2006a). For example, many news critics bemoan the journalistic attempts to "balance" coverage of the controversy over whether global warming has a man-made component. Though it is a contentious political issue, the scientific consensus (a few dissenters notwithstanding) is that humans are indeed responsible for the increase in average temperatures over the last several decades.

All of the above mutations of the core norms can be explained, at least in part, by the financial constraints under which journalists operate. For example, deadline pressure and the need to keep costs low make relying on eagerto-be-heard officials a tempting alternative to original research and verification. Turning now to those constraints, it is clear that an understanding of them provides a wealth of knowledge about how political reality is whittled down to a daily news product.

FINANCIAL CONSTRAINTS IN JOURNALISM

The American press's for-profit status burdens the craft of political journalism in numerous ways. Several well-known patterns of political news can be deduced from two primary financial mandates: (1) the need to produce as inexpensive a product as feasible, and (2) the need to generate revenue.

In the broadest sense, the need to keep costs low means using the fewest possible resources for the shortest period of time. This produces tight deadlines, small staffs with low salaries (print journalism is one of the lowest paid occupations that requires a bachelor's degree), minimal equipment budgets, and so on. One of the most consequential implications of this is the fact that journalists give favorable consideration to news that is produced for them. One of the most time-and-resource-scarce modes, local television news too often carries this to an extreme by airing Video News Releases (VNRs). These are press releases meant to look like local news packages, complete with voice-over scripts for the local anchors to read, when in fact they are produced by corporations or government agencies to promote products or push a policy agenda. Use of VNRs in local television news is rampant and often undisclosed to viewers (Farsetta and Price 2006). In the political realm, press conferences, press releases, VNRs, events held in proximity to news organization headquarters, and so on, all make the journalist's job easier and less expensive, and thus stand a strong chance of appearing in the news relatively unfiltered. This privileges actors who possess the skills and resources to produce such *news-influencing activity*. It is also one of many explanations for the official-sources bias.

The other side of the financial ledger is the need to generate revenue. Very little revenue comes directly from customers, as broadcast television costs nothing to consume, and subscriptions bring in just the fraction of the cash needed to operate a cable news operation or newspaper. It would thus appear that the need to attract sponsors is paramount to this mandate. As sponsorship rates are calibrated to audience size, however, the bulk of the attention is turned to cultivating as large an audience as possible. The consultant-driven world of audience maximization results in several classic news-judgment criteria, found in any introductory journalism textbook. Though these and many other criteria apply to all news, the following are especially helpful for explicating the predictable tenor of the political news product.

First, audiences tend to prefer news that is *colorful* and *dramatic*. Television news is particularly wrought with the "if it bleeds, it leads" mentality (see Rosenstiel, et. al. 2007, ch. 3). At times, it seems as though the sole news judgment criteria of large-market local news are the body count of the incident and whether they were able to obtain compelling video. "Drama" refers to a preference for stories that fit the basic dramatic structure: exposition, the initial complication, rising tension building to a climax, and finally a resolution.

The O. J. Simpson affair of 1994–1995 fit the dramatic narrative perfectly. Besides having large doses of sex, violence, and celebrity, it garnered sustained saturation coverage for more than a year because it flowed like an exceptionally long episode of the television show *Law and Order*: First the bodies were found. Then the detectives began their work, leading quickly to pegging the husband as the lead suspect. The plot twisted with the slow-speed car chase seen live on national television, and then the suspect was quickly apprehended. The long trial began, with dueling personalities and unexpected turns. Finally, the climax was reached with the "we the jury find the defendant. . ." pronouncement. Every day brought a new development, however trivial, that could be parlayed into a news hook. Soon a veritable O.J. industrial complex sprung up, in which ever-increasing resources were poured into the story until news organizations had a vested interest in keeping it going.

On the political front, scandals obviously come closest to having an O.J.-like perfect storm of newsworthiness. The actual importance of a scandal to the public or to the institutions of governance is secondary in news judgment to its sexiness. Also, election cycles fit the dramatic-narrative criterion better than static issue deliberation, no matter how potentially consequential to the news consumer. Of course, certain aspects of election cycles are more newsworthy than others—a point discussed in the next section.

Another classic criterion is *timeliness*. Given the short attention span of the American news audience, journalists feel tremendous pressure not to dwell on a topic for an extended time period, unless it produces a constant flow of new information. Again, election cycles are particularly amenable to this criterion, as coverage-hungry candidates keep journalists well fed with a constant stream of statements.

While being new brings coverage to a phenomenon, being *novel* is even better. The unusual is always privileged over the routine. The old adage is that "man bites dog" will win out every time over its less novel counterpart, "dog bites man." The problem is that much of politics is routine. Just as the plane that lands safely fails to make news, so too do the ever-present Americans in poverty, or the (allegedly) ever-declining moral fabric of society. No matter how important a perennial issue is to a large constituency, it will not make news without a news hook.

Finally, *proximity* garners privilege over distance. Local news focuses on local events first, then the state, then the nation. The national news focuses on America first. Though most people would find this to be appropriate, it can lead to parochialism, ethnocentrism, and the ignoring of seemingly distant stories that in fact have important implications for the United States. For example, two events in the mid 1990s—the distant aftermath of the Soviet Union's invasion of Afghanistan and the Sudanese civil war—played a key role in Osama bin Laden's rise to power.

Beyond the textbook news judgment criteria are several other patterns that stem from financial constraints. First, the public not only has a limited attention span, it is perceived also to carry a limited capacity for the absorption of complex concepts. The news therefore must be kept *simple*. This disadvantages inherently complex political phenomena such as monetary policy, as well as aspects of issues that require abstract reasoning (such as causal arguments), no matter how important to the lives of the audience.

Another observed tendency is *moderatism* (Gans 1979). Though the mainstream media might not favor the left or the right, they certainly favor the center. Public opinion sets the boundaries outside of which the news product will not veer, for fear of losing audience or appearing to push a radical agenda.

Several of the above factors combine to form one of the most important observations about political news: it tends to be *episodic*—meaning news stories emphasize "concrete events"—rather than thematic—meaning an emphasis on "general outcomes or conditions" (Iyengar 1991, 14). The over-personalization, over-dramatization, and fragmentation of political news cause it to exist "in self-contained dramatic capsules, isolated from each other in time and space. The impression given by the news is of a jigsaw puzzle that is out of focus and missing many pieces" (Bennett 2005, 60). For example, night after night the local television news leads with "the following people were murdered in the metro area today. . ." However, seldom do they take a step back to ascertain the socio-economic causes of crime.

INDEPENDENT MEDIA INFLUENCE:
THE CASE OF HORSE-RACE ELECTION COVERAGE

Independent media influence is an effect of the press on any political actor or process that is attributable to the unique organizational norms and constraints of American media institutions, and not to actors or phenomena external to the news organization. The domain of elections provides a perfect illustration of the myriad processes that produce this power.

The universe of potentially newsworthy events in an election is vast. For each of the many simultaneous races, two or more viable candidates make daily speeches, hold press conferences, and issue press releases. They also have dozens (congressional) or hundreds (presidential) of paid staffers and volunteers mobilized to raise money and awareness for their candidacy. Also, polls are released throughout the campaign season, affected by high-profile gaffes, strategy, external events, and the idiosyncrasies of the public. Most important, at least from a democratic-theoretical perspective, the candidates have a general ideology, a partisan attachment (usually), positions on all issues, specific proposals for the most salient issues and for their pet issues, a constituency with its own needs and quirks, a political history, a biography, a family, and a distinct "character."

There is an unmistakable pattern as to which of those phenomena tend to make news. One of the biggest complaints about political news is the overemphasis of most campaign coverage on the "horse race"—poll standings and campaign strategy—at the expense of substantive issue coverage of the kind that would help voters make informed electoral choices. Though there is much discussion of the consequences of such coverage (Patterson 1994), it is also instructive to ask *why* it dominates the election news landscape. The norms and constraints of professional journalism offer numerous insights into this puzzle.

First, the contemporary rendering of objectivity as passivity/neutrality suggests that political journalists privilege objective-sounding poll numbers over critical examination of the policy consequences of the candidates' platforms. "It has been a bad week for George Bush" need not be a biased statement, if it is backed up with numbers from a respected professional poll. On the other hand, "George Bush's tax plan doesn't add up," even if corroborated by an expert, is a dangerous path for bias-averse journalists to take. By the same token, the following typical lead sentence from the 2004 election is at once completely safe and uninformative: "Democratic presidential candidate John Kerry completed a post-convention swing through Ohio yesterday at a rally outside a pizza parlor where he delivered a message of family values and jobs to a crowd hungry for change" (Eaton 2004). Had the article made some attempt to critique the implications or feasibility of Kerry's jobs proposal, rather than simply parroting his talking points, it would have (1) given swing voters a concrete tidbit of knowledge to aid their decision making, but (2) run afoul of the perceived neutrality mandate.

Also, deadlines, limited resources, and the limited expertise of most political journalists render horse race coverage easier to execute than in-depth issue coverage. The nuances of budgeting and foreign policy, if not beyond the reach of the reporters who happen to be assigned to the political beat, are certainly perceived to be beyond the reach of the audience on whom they depend. Finally, the need for audience maximization makes the flashy, dynamic sports frame more appealing than dry, stagnant issue analysis. The numbers change every day; the candidates' positions on particular issues usually do not. Thus the horse race can be presented as a series of episodes of a dramatic narrative with a clear beginning, daily candidate statements, unexpected complications amid a schedule of exciting events, and a steady build to a climax—election-day evening.

Together, these elements of the filter work to warp the entire universe of potentially newsworthy campaign phenomena into a horse race. *This is independent media influence: an effect on a political process attributable to the unique organizational attributes of the political news media.*

SPURIOUS MEDIA INFLUENCE

Recognition of true media influence demands adherence to basic causal logic, in that we must rule out other potential causes that render such power spurious. Gross media influence in politics—that is, the measured or presumed effect of news content on the political process—is attenuated to the extent that news content is driven by one of two varieties of input: (1) tangible, measurable elements of political reality that are external to the news-making process, or (2) conscious attempts by political actors or other elites to manipulate the news.

Figure 2.2 outlines the causal logic of news content in light of this premise. On the right-hand side of both diagrams, news content affects a political phenomenon—the "media effect" from Figure 2.1. But the causal character of this effect depends crucially on what is driving the news content. In the top diagram, the effective antecedent to the news-politics relationship is the news organization itself. In other words, the quirks of the news-making process are solely responsible for shaping the news content, and thus any effect of such content is attributable to the press as a political institution. In the bottom diagram, however, tangible external phenomena and/or elite rhetoric find their way into the news product relatively unfiltered. To the extent that this happens, the external reality or elite rhetoric is the effective antecedent to the news-politics relationship, rendering the power of news spurious (see Leighley 2004 for a framework that utilizes similar insights). Each of the two influence-attenuating factors is explored in detail.

External Reality

The media potentially affect the political process with every word that they publish or broadcast. If nothing else, they are typically the public's primary or sole source of information about any given political phenomenon. To the

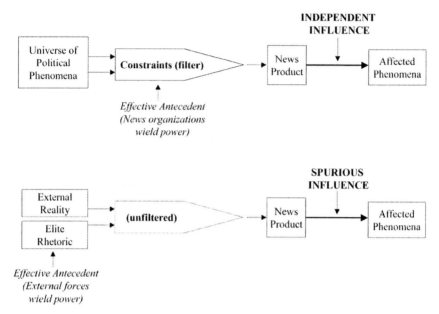

Figure 2.2. The Causal Logic of News Content

extent that they succeed in holding a mirror to the political world, however, then their effect on politics would be merely as an information carrier. They would transmit information, perhaps condensed, but not distorted in any discernable, politically important sense, with which citizens can make informed choices. As Walter Lippman noted long ago, "Were reporting the simple recovery of obvious facts, the press agent would be little more than a clerk" (1997, 218).

This "clerk" effect is not the type of effect that occupies the thoughts and projects of most media scholars and democratic theorists. In the immediate aftermath of World War II radio propaganda, scholars worried about pernicious effects of elite-controlled mass communication (Lazarsfeld, Berelson, Gaudet 1948). More recently, activists and a few academics have complained about a liberally biased press and the resulting damage to informed deliberation, while a larger group of academics documents and laments the press's enforcement of capitalist/corporatist values at the expense of alternative viewpoints. Also, much contemporary inquiry asks how the professional norms and routines of news organizations affect the quality of discourse by excluding certain issues from the table, and by reducing complex issues to their colorful, oversimplified, and ultimately salable elements.

A common thread in most of these projects is a concern with *divergence*. Independent media influence is wielded only to the extent that the news product diverges from tangible, agreed-upon reality, if there is one. Take crime for example. Local television news stokes fear, paranoia, and racial distrust through its all-consuming obsession with violent crime. However, if the crime rate were such that every citizen of a community faced a high likelihood of being violated on a given day, so much so that all citizens would rate it as their primary concern in life (in a theoretical opinion poll untainted by crime news), then suddenly terms such as "obsession" and "paranoia" would no longer describe the tenor of local news. Also, to be absurdly counterfactual for a moment, imagine that every African-American male really did pose an imminent violent threat to every white citizen. Then it would be specious to blame the *press* for sowing racial distrust. Obviously, though, critics argue that the importance appointed to the crime issue dwarfs its actual importance in society, however measured, and that African Americans bear a disproportionate brunt of this coverage (Dixon and Linz 2000). A longitudinal perspective shows direct evidence of one aspect of the disconnect: While crime dropped nationwide during the 1990s, the proportion of television news devoted to crime increased over the same time period (Lowry, Ching, Nio, and Leitner 2003). Thus it is the disconnect between external phenomena and news coverage thereof that gives crime coverage its ability to scare citizens needlessly into a fortress mentality.

Given the fundamental linguistic contestation inherent in politics, of course, many political domains have no agreed-upon reality baseline. After all, Lippman's "clerk" comment was merely a setup for his contention that "in respect to most of the big topics of news, the facts are not simple, and not at all obvious, but subject to choice and opinion. . ." (218). For example, what *should* be the tone of abortion coverage? Should it be evenly balanced between the two sides? Should it defer to state-of-the-art scientific knowledge? Pinning an external reality on the issue would be an epistemological absurdity. On the other hand, to the extent that the tone of economic coverage follows changes in objective economic indicators month by month (chapter 4), or that variation in the amount of coverage granted to foreign conflicts is a function of the actual intensity of the conflict (chapter 5), it is fair to say that the reality baseline is dictating coverage, and that the press's independent influence over this issue area is attenuated by the news media's faithful mirroring of reality.

Elite Influence

The second broad category of power attenuation is the attempt by political elites to sway news coverage in their favor. It is well understood that public officials, interest groups, and other players expend tremendous resources attempting to influence the news product. To the extent that these efforts are successful in a given context, the media fail to wield independent power in any meaningful sense. As Schudson (2002) puts it, "Media power looms large if the portrait of the world the media present to audiences stems from the preferences and perceptions of publishers, editors, and reporters unconstrained by democratic controls. However, if the media typically mirror the views and voices of established (and democratically selected) government officials, then the media are more nearly the neutral servants of a democratic order." Unlike the reality baseline, which applies to a limited number of political domains, elite influence is pervasive in all aspects of politics. The question of who sets the press's agenda, therefore, usually boils down to a game between norm-and-finance-constrained journalists and elites in search of favorable publicity.

NOTE

1. I heard the rain analogy from *Fort Worth Star-Telegram* editorial writer and columnist Jack Z. Smith at an academic panel, who in turn attributed it to Stuart Long, a longtime Texas journalist.

Chapter Three

The Theory of
Conditional Media Influence

In what political domains does the press wield its greatest power? And when does it cede the power to shape its product to external actors or events? This chapter builds a theory of conditional media influence. Specifically, the task is to explain variation in the amount of independent media influence in a political domain.

PRINCIPLES

Following the conceptual framework set forth in the last chapter, *media influence* is defined as the independent capacity of news organizations, in reducing the universe of political phenomena to a discrete news product, to affect public opinion, constrain the behavior of candidates, officeholders, and other elite political actors, or influence policy output. To be *independent*, the effect must derive from the unique organizational attributes of the press, and not from reality or elite influence. Finally, a *political domain* is any single set of issues, processes, or phenomena over which news content potentially wields influence.

The theory begins with a first principle: *News organizations endeavor to produce a product that is consistent with their core norms to the greatest feasible extent.* Though the political news product seldom resembles one that would be made with only the core norms in mind, they nonetheless serve as a good baseline for the theory. After all, journalists have a compelling stake in shaping the news, to the greatest extent allowable, according to their core norms: providing a product, independent from faction, that effectively

21

monitors power and truthfully relays the facts that facilitate informed self-governance. News organizations incur a cost—in their perception of their product's value—by deviating from these norms.

The core norms are just an idealistic baseline, though. The other competing influences on political news (reality, elite influence, and the behavioral implications of the constraints and realistic norms) pull news content away from the core norms to a greater or lesser extent within a given domain. Two primary implications of this for media influence flow directly from the conceptual framework of chapter 2: (1) *The greater the pull toward external reality or elites, the more independent media influence is attenuated*; (2) *The greater the pull toward the constraints or realistic norms, the more independent media influence is enhanced.*

The key question becomes what pulls the news product toward one or more of the competing influences in a particular domain? A straightforward economic proposition sets the table for the answer: *News is pulled toward a competing influence to the extent that the cost of ignoring the influence outweighs the cost of deviating from the core norms.*

HYPOTHESES

The final step, then, is to hypothesize the conditions under which each competing factor might portend a relatively higher cost for news organizations, depending on how they cover the domain. The first hypothesis is the key to understanding how, when, and why news organizations wield influence; the other three predict the conditions under which external forces push their way into the news product.

Invocation of Constraints Hypothesis: The media wield more influence when a greater number of organizational constraints vary meaningfully in the domain.

Each constraint derives from either a deeply ingrained journalistic norm or an unavoidable financial or logistical concern. The larger the variance in the extent to which characteristics of a domain are amenable to the constraint, the greater the normative or financial stake news organizations have in shaping the news toward the favorable characteristics. Therefore, the larger the number of constraints that are invoked in a domain, and the more they meaningfully vary, the more the news product likely diverges from reality and elite influence, and thus the more independent influence the press wields.

For instance, why do some Senate hearings receive coverage while others are ignored? To use real examples, some hearings deal with homeland security, while others concern "the consolidation of jurisdictional functions of the SEC and CFTC," or "contractor accountability at DOE facilities." It is easy to see that the characteristics of this domain (the individual hearings) vary wildly in their potential appeal to a news audience. Clearly, readership would suffer if the *Washington Post* focused more on Department of Energy personnel matters than on homeland security. Thus the news judgment criteria of color and drama are "invoked," meaning they exert a cost on news organizations that stray from them. On the other hand, a researcher might ask which senators are better able to garner coverage about homeland security issues. As the issue is held constant, color and drama would not be invoked.

Concrete Reality Hypothesis: A more concrete reality baseline attenuates media influence.

A domain has a "concrete reality" to the extent that its meaning, as constructed and understood by relevant actors, consists of a set of phenomena, the essential characteristics of which are (1) agreed upon by all actors involved, including journalists, the public, and participants spanning the diversity of relevant interests, and (2) are readily perceivable and interpretable by journalists. Of course, as these are tough conditions to meet absolutely, no political domain would ever qualify as entirely concrete. Nonetheless, domains differ meaningfully enough with respect to these criteria to enable differentiation along this dimension.

The more the domain is shaped by a concrete reality, the higher the credibility costs would be for news organizations to create a product that deviates from the reality, and the more deviating would violate the norm of faithful, factual reporting. Lippman (1997) argued that "only. . . where social conditions take recognizable and measurable shape. . . [are] the tests of news sufficiently exact to make the charges of perversion or suppression more than a partisan judgment" (218). The contemporary corollary, given the abundance of watchdog groups, academics, blogs, angry subscriber/letter-writers, and other "tests of news," is that only when social conditions *do not* take a recognizable shape are journalists free to distort and suppress in accordance with their norms and constraints.

An example of a perfectly concrete reality—albeit from outside of politics—is retrospective reporting of the weather. Television meteorologists are entirely constrained by the reliable, respected technologies of thermometers, barometers, and rain gauges. Telling the public that it reached 90 degrees today, when the readily perceivable temperature on any resident's backyard thermometer was 65, would be tremendously costly for a reporter's credibility. Thus, variation in retrospective weather reports is explained entirely by the real weather, and meteorologists act as mere information carriers in this domain (which, of course, is their goal).

At the other extreme is an issue such as abortion. Adversaries fail to agree even on what the central issue is (the life of the fetus? Women's autonomy?), or on the definition of core concepts such as "life." They are not helped by scientific consensus, which has shifted the definition of a viable life over the years. The press, therefore, is unconstrained by a concrete reality in this domain, and is free to frame the issue in whatever normatively or financially expedient manner it pleases.

Elite Consensus Hypothesis: An elite consensus attenuates media influence.

The greater the extent to which elites—at least those to which the press is known to index the tenor of its coverage—share a common vision of how the domain should be covered, the more they are able to act as a unified force pulling news content in their direction. Going against an elite consensus creates risk for journalists who depend on those elites for access. Though a true elite consensus is rare within the most common domains of Washington controversy, if the party in power is particularly adept at framing its message or intimidating dissenters, it can nonetheless exercise a large degree of control over the news (see Bennett, Lawrence, and Livingston 2007, Entman 2004). Actors in a truly conflictual elite, on the other hand, cancel each other out. If news organizations stand to catch flack from one side or the other no matter how they cover the issue, then there is no differential cost to covering it one way as opposed to another.

Elite Salience Hypothesis: The higher the stakes for the involved elites, the more successfully they will attenuate media influence.

Skilled elites know how to reduce the cost of news production through press releases, press-ready events, and regular, predictable contact with beat reporters. Though these news-management techniques give elites a measure of control over their press image, they also require the use of limited time and financial resources, and their excessive use can trigger a backlash from independence-conscious journalists. A motivated elite, therefore, should be more likely to employ the skills and resources necessary to sway the news product.

Though elites seemingly hold stake in any domain in which they bother to be involved, meaningful variance nonetheless can be observed in issue salience. For example, it is reasonable to infer that, to elected officeholders, the domain of elections—specifically their own—would be of the highest salience. Also, an issue that defines particular officeholders—their marquee proposal, their trademark issue, one in which their involvement bears large consequences (intentionally or not) for their career advancement—should garner more of their attention and resources. For instance, as the prosecution of a war holds the potential as high as any issue to define a presidency, we can expect a greater allotment of media-control resources to a war than to a circuit court appointment or a trade pact.

THEORY MEETS DATA

The remaining chapters serve as three self-contained illustrations of the conceptual framework. By modeling systematic variation in the political news product in three distinct domains of substantive political interest, much will be learned about the contours of media influence in the political process.

In addition, taken as a whole, the three chapters form a test of the theory of media influence. The three studies are designed to vary along the key theoretical dimensions—concreteness of reality, elite consensus and salience, and invocation of constraints. Chapter four examines *New York Times* coverage of the economy, a realm with a highly concrete reality, conflicted political elites, and relatively little constraint invocation. Additional nuance is added by measuring the economy along two dimensions with variable concreteness. Chapter five explores *Times* coverage of foreign conflicts, a domain with a fairly concrete but difficult to perceive reality, a unified and motivated elite, and seemingly meaningful variation in one notable journalistic constraint. Finally, chapter six deals with print and television coverage of Supreme Court decisions, a domain with little reality baseline, a motivated elite, and high invocation of several important journalistic constraints.

Chapter Four

Economic News

Late in the 1996 presidential campaign, Republican nominee Bob Dole tried to deny a concrete reality. Unable to change the subject from the stellar economy—a clear winning issue for his incumbent opponent Bill Clinton—he turned the issue on its head by asserting that the U.S. economy was in its worst shape in a century (Lewis 1996).

As he found out, though, the boundaries within which elites can shape public discourse are set in part by the reality baselines that define a political domain. Even in the midst of its "he said/she said" campaign routines, the press refused to give uncritical play to a demonstrably incorrect statement. Dole's comment was thus relegated to snide opinion articles and talking-head commentary.

The economy, then, provides a fitting first test of conditional media influence. This chapter models monthly variation in the tone of economic news on the *New York Times* front page from 1980–1996. The three classes of news product influences serve as independent variables to determine the extent of true and spurious media influence in the economic domain. Additionally, the concrete reality hypothesis is tested by parsing economic news into two distinct components of varying reality hardness.

As political variables go, the aggregate state of the economy is a highly concrete reality. Objective numerical indicators of it—most of which are highly correlated with each other—are made public at regular intervals. The primary limitation on its hardness is that differently motivated actors can employ different indicators to serve their agendas. The ambiguity inhering from multiple measures of economic conditions, however, actually benefits this study by serving as leverage to test the concrete reality hypothesis.

Another limitation is that not every person experiences the same economic reality. Blunt indicators such as GDP growth measure whether the pie is growing, but they fail to tap who is benefiting from the growth. Given the dramatic widening of the gap between the rich and poor in America since the late 1970s, this concern may become more salient in political science treatments of the economy (see Sherman 2007 for evidence of the growing gap). For now, though, I follow previous uses of standard economic indicators in political science—in studies of news, electoral forecasting, public opinion, and so on—as valid indicators of concrete macroeconomic reality.

DEPENDENT VARIABLES:
TWO TYPES OF ECONOMIC NEWS

This chapter examines economic news coverage in the *New York Times* from 1980 to 1996.[1] Previous studies that have grappled with the determinants of economic news tone (Nadeau, et. al., 1999, Mutz 1992, De Boef and Kellstedt 2004, Soroka 2006) measure tone along a single dimension, typically favorable/unfavorable.[2] Arguing that the singular favorability assessment is incomplete, I propose two distinct tone categories: *underlying conditions* and *episodes*. A *condition* is a judgment of the overall state of the economy, as typified in this December, 1991, article:

> The thousands of jobs being trimmed from the nation's work force by. . . major corporations are never coming back, executives say. That is the single biggest difference between *the current economic slump* and previous recessions. "*The recession was a lot worse than we thought*, and it triggered this round of cutbacks," said George Davis. "But if it were just *the recession*," he said, "we would be hiring these people back again. And we aren't going to do that." (Lohr 1991, emphasis added).

"Recession" is the most common but not the only cue for a negative *conditions* code. Favorable *conditions*, on the other hand, bring phrases such as " in these *good times*" and "Greenspan worries that the *booming economy* might trigger inflation."

Distinct from the *underlying condition* evaluation is the *episode*. Roughly analogous to an "episodic" news frame (Iyengar 1991, and see chapter 2), this refers to the specific development that triggered the article's publication—the actual "news" in the news story. Consider the lead sentence from this September 1996, story: "*Household income rose in 1995* for the first time in six years, the Census Bureau reported today, as *the number of poor people in the United States dropped by more than 1.6 million*, reaching historic lows for blacks and the elderly" (Holmes 1996, emphasis added). The innovation that precipitated the story's production—the rise in household income—clearly is good news.

Why is it important to separate the two? Consider this lead sentence from November 1991: "The appetite for American goods and services remains robust around the globe, a sign that exports are likely to remain a bright spot in the otherwise lackluster American economy" (Nasar 1991). In this case, the news hook is clearly good (a robust appetite for American goods) whereas "lackluster American economy" is a negative assessment of the economy's condition. A unidimensional coding scheme likely would defer to the news hook in this case, rendering this story "good news."[3] It seems wise, however, to consider the potential effect of yet another story mentioning the 1991 recession—an effect that would be washed out in a single "favorable/unfavorable" code.

Most importantly, the use of two coverage measures enables a direct test of the concrete reality hypothesis. To do this, I argue that *conditions* represent a more concrete reality than *episodes*. On the one hand, the tone of assessments of the overall state of the economy signifies a stable, composite attitude about the economy, based on agreed-upon and readily available indicators. The observation of a recession or boom has considerable inertia and momentum, and cannot be challenged or altered impetuously without great credibility costs to the journalist or officeholder attempting to do so.

In contrast, though more positive *episodes* are likely to occur during booms than hard times (and vice-versa) we nonetheless should expect potentially newsworthy good *and* bad events in all but the most extreme months, thus leaving more room for editorial judgment. Though the composite tone of *episodes* that end up in the news should still follow the real economy, the pattern likely will be far more jagged, with larger fluctuations between single months. The decision to cover any given event—the release of new economic numbers, and so forth—is not as obviously tied to any agreed-upon reality, and thus should be subject to more independent news judgment. By the same logic, *episodes* should be more susceptible to elite influence than *conditions*. For example, Bob Dole likely could have stayed within the realm of plausibility by citing a single indicator to argue that the economy might be heading in the wrong direction, rather than making a bold (and bald) assertion about its general health.

This leads to the specific manifestation of the concrete reality hypothesis for this chapter: reality should exert heavier constraint on coverage of *conditions* than on coverage of *episodes*. Specifically, objective economic indicators should correlate more highly with *conditions* coverage than *episodes*. Conversely, elite and independent media influence should be stronger in the presence of *episode* coverage's softer reality baseline.

MEASURING ECONOMIC REALITY

If economic reality constrains coverage on account of its concreteness, as hypothesized, then the dependent variables should be highly correlated with accepted objective measures of economic health. Further, any correlation should be more pronounced for *conditions* than for *episodes*.

The dynamics of economic reality have many indicators, most of which tend to be correlated with each other. Table 4.1 shows the bivariate correlations between coverage and various economic indicators. Included are typical measures such as the Consumer Price Index and unemployment, as well as measures of their *change* by month (inflation and unemployment change, respectively). Also included are the *changes* in three common composite indicators: the indexes of leading, coincident, and lagging indicators.

The results clearly show the closer adherence to reality of the coverage type that represents a more concrete reality baseline. For all indicators for which at least one correlation is significant, the correlation with *conditions* is higher than that for *episodes*. Some differences are striking, such as that for unemployment and the index of lagging indicators. Though others perhaps are too close to declare a statistically meaningful difference, the overall pattern clearly did not occur by chance.

Hereafter, economic reality is represented by an economy scale consisting of three correlated economic indicators: leading indicators change, coincident indicators change, and change in unemployment.

A visual examination lends further insight into the differences between *conditions* and *episodes*. Figures 4.1 and 4.2 show the similarities between coverage and the economy scale. The greater amount of momentum and inertia in *conditions* coverage than in *episodes* is clear from the fact that *conditions* crosses the zero mark—denoting a change from net positive to net negative coverage over a single month—fewer than one-third as many times as

Table 4.1.   Bivariate Correlations between Coverage and Various Economic Indicators

	Conditions	Episodes
CPI	.239*	.071
Inflation	−.109	−.110
Unemployment	−.492*	−.135
Unemployment Change	−.363*	−.270*
Leading Indicators Change	.047	.133
Lagging Indicators Change	.468*	.213*
Coincident Indicators Change	.337*	.290*

N = 193
Note: *p<.05

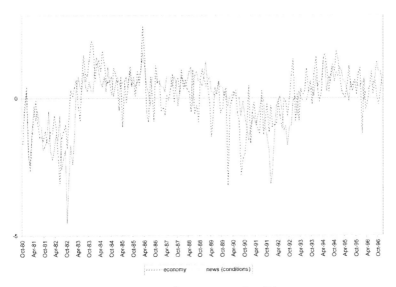

Figure 4.1. Comparing Coverage to the Economy: Conditions

episodes. While the general state of the economy does not change radically from month to month, the changes therein are more subject to jumping from good news, in the aggregate, to bad news. As a result *conditions* adheres more closely to the economic scale than *episodes*, despite the fact that the scale is composed of three measures of change in economic indicators.

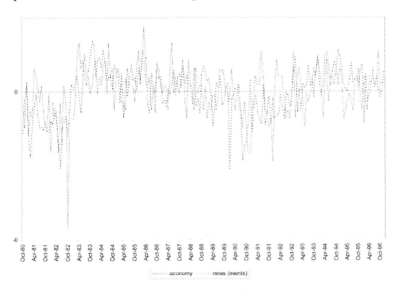

Figure 4.2. Comparing Coverage to the Economy: Episodes

MEDIA INFLUENCE IN THE ECONOMIC REALM

Though the correlation between economic coverage and the true economy is considerable, much variation in news remains to be explained, especially for *episodes* coverage. First, the question of the timeliness of economic reporting aroused much attention in the 1990s from scholars and especially from bitter Republicans. Hetherington (1996) lends scholarly credence to partisan complaints after the 1992 presidential election by showing that the overwhelming negative tone of economic news, which belied the incipient recovery, moved voters toward Clinton. Hetherington's study relies on inference: coverage was assumed to be predominantly negative. Indeed, figure 4.1 shows a considerable dip in *conditions* news from April to October of 1992, even as the indicators were on the upswing. Nonetheless, it is useful to ask whether his findings generalize to a broad pattern of coverage lag. On the one hand, the norm of covering politics comprehensively and truthfully turns uncertainty into risk for reporters. Perhaps a month or two of indicators must accrue before reporters are willing to say with confidence that the economy really has reversed course. On the other hand, the mandate for timeliness, as well as the efficiency with which governmental and private agencies communicate information about economic conditions, could minimize this concern.

To test for a lag in coverage, table 4.2 models coverage as a function of the economic reality scale at various month-interval lags. First, *conditions* coverage appears to be predicted about as well by the contemporaneous economy as by the month prior, while further lags fail to impact. A lag of at most one month fails to be compelling evidence of a general coverage lag. After all, potentially newsworthy information released during the last week of a month might not be published until the first week of the next month.

Table 4.2.   Predicting Coverage with the Economic Scale at Various Lags

	Conditions		Episodes	
	B	SE	B	SE
Economic Scale	.28*	.11	.17*	.10
Scale, lag 1	.35*	.12	.25*	.10
Scale, lag 2	.01	.12	.23*	.10
Scale, lag 3	.01	.12	.05	.10
Lagged Coverage	.74*	.05	.17*	.07
Constant	−.33	.23	−.63*	.19
Adjusted R-squared	.70		.22	
N	191		191	

Note: OLS regression; coefficients are unstandardized. *p<.05

On the other hand, the first two lags of the economy scale wield a statistically significant influence over *episodes* coverage, each of a marginally higher effect than the current month. Though it may seem puzzling that the culmination of monthly events would be reported with a lag, it comports nicely with expectations stated above that events coverage is where editorial judgment—including the hypothesized judgment of caution in economic reporting—is more apt to be exercised. Overall, evidence of a general lag in economic coverage, especially of a length that could be of serious consequence to political discourse and processes, is weak.

The multivariate analysis presented later will enable a further test of whether uncertainty causes reporters to abate the intensity of their assessments until the economy has been trending in the same direction for a few months. A *trend* variable measures the number of months in which the economy has moved in the same direction without reversing course; in other words, for how many consecutive months the economic scale has carried the same sign. A positive result would indicate that news of economic health, positive or negative, becomes more emphatic as the economy stays its course, controlling for the actual level of the economic indicators.

Another journalistic constraint relevant to economic news is the preference for bad news over good news (see Harrington 1989), as news organizations should get more mileage out of stoking fears of layoffs than for congratulating the presidential administration on a job well done. Table 4.3 shows the average number of articles by month, broken down by whether the net tone of

Table 4.3. Average Amount of Coverage by Positive, Negative, or Neutral News Months

	Conditions			
	Articles	s.e.	t	N
Positive	4.1	.2		94
Neutral	2.3			23
Negative	8.0	.6	6.5*	78
	Episodes			
	Articles	s.e.	t	N
Positive	4.4	.3		64
Neutral	3.8			36
Negative	6.8	.5	4.1*	95

Notes: Articles = average number of articles per month, for months in which the net tone of news is positive, negative, or exactly neutral.
N = number of months in data set that fall into that category.
t = t-test for difference in mean amounts of coverage between positive and negative news months. Equal variances not assumed.
*p <.05

news that month was good, bad, or neutral. For *conditions* coverage, bad news months enjoy twice the coverage of good news months. *Episodes* coverage also slants toward bad news, with a premium of around 50 percent for bad news over good news. Interestingly, neutral news months—arguably the dullest from the standpoint of newsworthiness—receive the lowest amount of coverage.

The number of months that fall into each category also tells an interesting tale about news judgment, consistent with the concrete reality hypothesis. For *conditions*, almost twenty more months carried a positive tone than negative. With the less concrete reality baseline of *episodes* coverage, however, the coverage tilted toward the negative side, with around thirty more bad months than good months. With no *a priori* expectation that *episodes* should be inherently more negative than *conditions*, this intriguing pattern likely results from the editorial freedom to choose more negative event stories.

ELITE INFLUENCE

In the conceptual framework, "elite influence" generally means the attempts of governmental officials to manipulate news content. The economic domain, however, suggests a broader rendering of elites. Various non-governmental actors, most notably leaders in the business community, give pronouncements about the state of the economy that are taken seriously by expert-reliant news organizations. In their model of the flow between economic reality, news, and public opinion, Nadeau and others (1999) include a measure of the tone of business elites' prospective and retrospective economic evaluations from a Conference Board survey. They find retrospective evaluations to be a powerful predictor of coverage.

Similarly, I include in the full model the marginals of two survey questions from the Livingston Survey, a long-running poll of economic experts from the government, industry, and academics.[4] The survey asks the experts to predict levels of several economic indicators, both contemporaneously but before they are released, and a given number of months into the future. To tap a reality most similar to that in the model, I rely on two questions that forecast Gross Domestic Product levels, of which I take the first difference to represent predicted levels of GDP growth. To tap retrospective evaluations, I use their prediction of current GDP levels. For prospective evaluations, I use their prediction of levels two quarters ahead.[5]

Though business elites undoubtedly disagree over certain aspects of economic health, it is not likely that their perception of *specific* indicators is subject to Bob Dole–like projection bias, as their primary motivation does not stem from such an essential political bias as partisanship. The elite consensus hypothesis therefore predicts that those elites, to the extent that they diverge from reality for whatever reason, should enjoy considerable success at sway-ing news content. Also, the concrete reality hypothesis predicts that their suc-cess should be greater for *episodes* coverage than for *conditions*.

On the other hand, the theory portends trouble for governmental elites try-ing to influence news. Though surely all political elites have at least some sense of the true economic conditions, their divergent incentives to spin that information set them at polar opposites. As the president's party typically takes credit for a good economy and the blame for a bad one, he and his party have a strong incentive to frame the economy in as positive a light as is fea-sible. Likewise, the opposition party endeavors to put a negative spin on the economy, sometimes to Bob Dole–like excess. Given that neither actor enjoys dominance over the issue to the extent that the president does over foreign policy, the elite consensus hypothesis predicts that these countervailing mes-sages will prevent either from influencing news.

A preliminary examination of elite rhetoric shows the difficulty in even measuring variation in presidential mentions of the economy, as they are al-most uniformly positive, and wholly unrelated to the actual state of the econ-omy. For example, bivariate correlations between the economy scale and the number of times in a given month the president or his spokespersons utter certain clearly valenced economic phrases are all null ("recession" = $-.16$; "boom" = $.04$; "expansion" = $.02$). The number of recession mentions ranged from 0 to 25, but was unrelated to actual economic conditions, and was related to the election cycle only in 1992, when Bush was forced to re-spond to relentless questions about the recession (which, ironically, had ended). The number of mentions of "boom" and "expansion" was effectively flat, ranging from 0 to around 5 with no apparent pattern.

To measure governmental elite attempts at influence, then, we must design indirect measures. Recall the implication of indexing theory (chapter 2) that negative coverage of an incumbent party/official can be predicted by the ex-tent of official opposition. Though no feasible exogenous measure exists of opposition rhetoric, I conducted a content analysis of the *New York Times* in search of congressional leaders from the opposition party attempting to make economic news. The result is a count of the number of stories per month in which the most high-profile opposition leader is mentioned in an economic context.[6] This, of course, is not an exogenous measure of elite attempts at in-fluence, as it measures only the number of *successful* attempts to make news. Thus it is unknown whether this truly measures elite attempts to influence the news or editorial judgment that the statements of opposition leaders are news-worthy. Nonetheless, it will be instructive to determine the conditions under which the presence of opposition statements is related to the tone of coverage.

Figure 4.3 shows the most striking pattern from the opposition leadership variable—Tip O'Neill's economy-related mentions during the Reagan years.

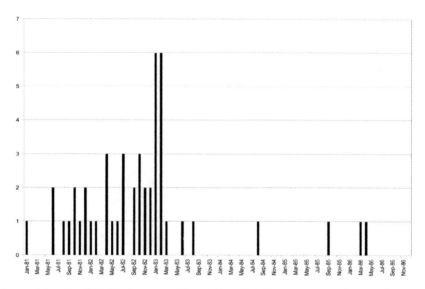

Figure 4.3.   Tip O'Neil's Economy-Related *New York Times* Mentions, by Month

Clearly, he was most vocal, or his vocalizations were most likely to be covered, during the recession. He either shut up, or was shut up by the Reagan-enamored press, during the later years of the administration.

Additionally, it is reasonable to posit that criticism of the economy—a proxy criticism of the president and his party—should be most vociferous around elections. On the other hand, Harrington (1989) finds economic coverage to be overly negative *except* during election years. These competing predictions are tested with a variable in the full model indicating whether the month is at the peak of election season.[7] Since the reality baseline sets the boundaries of the opposition's effectiveness, the variable includes only midterms, as the general political conditions are toughest for incumbent presidents in such elections (the period of analysis stops short of the aberrant 1998 midterm election).

FULL MODEL

I model the determinants of variation in economic coverage tone in the *New York Times* from 1980–1996 with OLS regression. Table 4.4 presents models with each type of elite economic assessment (retrospective and prospective) for each of the two varieties of coverage. Adding to the evidence from earlier tests, the full model further illustrates the hypothesized differences between the two types of coverage. Recall that elite influence should wield a larger effect over the less reality-constrained *episodes* coverage than *conditions* coverage.

Table 4.4. Modeling Economic News

	Conditions		Episodes		Conditions		Episodes	
	B	SE	B	SE	B	SE	B	SE
Conditions, lagged	.75*	.05	.22*	.07	.75*	.05	.20*	.07
Economy	.30*	.12	.21*	.10	.30*	.12	.20*	.10
Midterm	-.53	.96	-1.18	.79	-.39	.96	-.98	.79
Opposition leaders	-.29	.19	-.34*	.15	-.30	.19	-.35*	.15
Business elites, retrospective	.07	.06	.08	.05				
Business elites, prospective					.08	.05	.10*	.04
Trend	.12	.14	.17	.12	.11	.14	.14	.12
(Constant)	-.69	.53	-1.03*	.44	-.78	.50	-1.26*	.41
Adjusted R-squared	.69		.19		.69		.21	
N	193		193		193		193	

Note: OLS regression; coefficients are unstandardized. *p<.05

Turning first to economic elites, this project apparently will not add to the vigorous scholarly debate over whether prospective or retrospective economic evaluations influence political phenomena. Both measures of the tone of economic elites' assessments work with similar magnitude across the models.[8] As for the concrete reality hypothesis, the overall pattern is weakly suggestive of a greater effect in the *episodes* model, but not to any degree of statistical confidence.

Coverage fails to diverge to the negative side during midterm elections, consistent with the hypothesized weak effect of governmental elites over economic news. On the other hand, the finding is positive for the rhetoric of opposition leaders. Recall, however, that it is not clear whether this variable is measuring elite influence or editorial judgment. Regardless, it supports the concrete reality hypothesis, in that it better explains *episodes* than *conditions*.

Finally, the prospect of a general lag in coverage is weakened by the failure of the *trend* variable to affect coverage. Apparently, reporting does not become more emphatic as the economy stays its course.

DISCUSSION

This chapter augments the standard treatments of economic news by modeling two distinct forms of it: *underlying conditions* and *episodes*. In addition to providing a more nuanced examination of economic news, this parsing enables the first direct test of the theory of conditional media influence. Indeed, consistent with the theory, the more concrete reality of *conditions* constrains coverage to a greater degree than *episodes*, which are more amenable to editorial judgment.

This study also performed well as one piece in the larger test of the theory. The unusually clear and concrete reality baseline did indeed set strict boundaries for the tone of economic coverage. Little else moves economic news beyond this powerful effect, though relatively unified economic elites are able to do so. Also, the invocation of the audience-motivated news judgment criterion of preference for negativity indeed plays a role, while the idea of a lag in coverage—atheoretical, though much discussed in popular discourse and documented anecdotally—fails to generalize in any meaningful sense.

This was perhaps an easy test of whether a reality baseline has any effect on coverage. The next chapter employs a baseline that, while concrete, is more difficult to perceive and measure than the ubiquitous economic indicators. This will serve as a tougher test of whether external phenomena constrain motivated political actors and journalists.

APPENDIX

Dependent Variables

Stories were taken from the *New York Times* from October, 1980, to December, 1996. They were captured from the Lexis-Nexis Academic Universe database using the following query: *"U.S. economy" in headline or lead paragraph; and "Section A Page 1" in full text; or "1 Page 1" in full text.*

Stories were coded by two researchers along three dimensions: (1) relevance: does the story contain a substantial evaluation of the United States economy? If not, the story was discarded. (2) *underlying conditions*: good, mixed/neutral, or bad. (3) *episodes*: good, mixed/neutral, or bad. The two coders overlapped 128 coding choices, with 89 percent agreement. The data were aggregated by month for *conditions* and *episodes* by subtracting the number of good stories from the number of bad. As the dual classification is crucial not only to the data coding, but to the theory itself, the coding criteria are described in detail in the text.

Supplementary Variables

All economic data acquired from James Stimson in 2001 unless otherwise noted.

CPI—Consumer Price Index.
Inflation—Growth in CPI, previous 12 months.
Unemployment—Percent unemployed.
Unemployment Change—Change from previous month.
Leading Indicators Change—Index thereof, change from previous month.
Lagging Indicators Change—Index thereof, change from previous month.
Coincident Indicators Change—Index thereof, change from previous month.

Presidential Rhetoric: Recession/Boom/Expansion—I conducted a search of the Lexis-Nexis Political Transcripts database. Such data was available beginning in January 1989. First, I searched for all presidential remarks, or those by his official spokespersons, about the economy with the terms "[president's last name]," "White House," and "Economy" or "Economic." For "recession," I narrowed the search by seeking the term "Recession." For the broader terms, "boom" and "expansion," I used the query "boom" within five words of ("economy" or "economic"). The variables are counts of the number of mentions of each term by month.

Independent Variables (Full Model)

Economy (mean = 0, sd = 2.22, min/max = -5.81/6.88)—An additive scale composed of leading indicators change, coincident indicators change, and change in unemployment. Each indicator is standardized. Change in unemployment, being negatively correlated with the other two, is reversed. Finally, the three are added together.

Midterm—A dummy variable indicating the midterm campaign season (the four months leading up to the election).

Opposition Leaders (mean = .51, sd = 1.24, min/max = 0/11)—A Lexis-Nexis search of the number of times the main congressional opposition leader is quoted in an economically relevant *New York Times* story. A count was derived from the following query:

> *"Economy" in headline or lead paragraph; and "[name (last, and first if necessary)]" in full text.* Narrowed by: *"[name]" within 20 words of ("economy" or "economic" or "recession" or "boom" or "expansion" or "downturn" or "unemployment" or "inflation").*

Business Elites, Retrospective (mean = 7.93, sd = 4.28, min/max = −1.1/22.93)—Business elites' prediction of the Gross Domestic Product for the current quarter. I differenced it, and then divided it by ten for metric equivalence. From the Livingston Survey, available on the Federal Reserve Bank of Philadelphia website: <http://www.phil.frb.org/econ/liv/index.html>. Accessed February 2, 2003.

Business Elites, Prospective (mean = 8.04, sd = 4.85, min/max = −1.4/22.83)—Business elites' prediction of the Gross Domestic Product for two quarters ahead. I differenced it, and then divided it by ten for metric equivalence. From the Livingston Survey.

Trend (mean=.31, sd=1.77, min/max=−4/9)—A count of the number of months during which the economy has moved in the same direction without reversing course; in other words, for how many consecutive months the economic scale has carried the same sign.

NOTES

1. Though scholars debate whether the *Times* is an appropriate venue for measuring media effect on public opinion, its prestige and influence make it ideal for a project focused on norms and routines.

2. Harrington (1989) and Behr and Iyengar (1985) use a different method: amount of coverage received by each story about a specific indicator, predicted by the level of the indicator. De Boef and Kellstedt (2004) add a second dimension to their analy-

sis: the message source. The present critique holds for those studies as well. Fogarty (2005), the data-collection collaborator for this chapter, uses the same two-tiered dependent variable in his analysis.

3. See, for instance, the description of the coding scheme in Nadeau, et. al. (1999, 118).

4. A replication of the Nadeau (et al. 1999), measure would be ideal. But I was unable to obtain this data.

5. The quarterly data does not mesh perfectly with the monthly dependent variable; but no such monthly data exists.

6. Tip O'Neill, then James Wright, then Tom Foley, then Bob Dole, then Newt Gingrich. The number of mentions of each was far greater than any other contemporaneous congressional party leader.

7. The month is coded "1" if it is within four months of the 1982, 1986, 1990, or 1994 elections, "0" otherwise. Alternate specifications (available from the author upon request) with a longer time frame, as well as with all elections, yielded no positive results, while the variable as specified is correlated (bivariate) with coverage. This specification hunt adds an element of fairness, in that I predict null results.

8. The identical metrics and similar mean and variance of prospective and retrospective evaluations enable a direct comparison of their coefficients in otherwise identical models.

Chapter Five

Foreign Conflicts News

In 1992, a civil war festered in the small central African nation of Rwanda, far out of view of American citizens, media, and policy makers. The conflict received only two mentions in the *New York Times* that year, and one concerned a rare ape that was found shot to death in the forest, "apparently a victim of the civil war in this country" (Perlez 1992). Two years later, the ethnic tensions that fueled the relatively minor skirmish exploded into unparalleled chaos, in which several hundred thousand citizens were killed in the first two months. Not surprisingly, this genocide grabbed the world's attention, including the *New York Times*, whose 209 mentions of it that year anointed it as one of the most heavily covered civil wars in the 1990s after Bosnia and Somalia.

Though the explanation for the coverage surge seems obvious, less obvious but just as interesting is the question of why the original conflict received so little coverage. Do African nations suffer from a general dearth of attention from ethnocentric Western media? Did the United States government's lack of attention to it deem it unnewsworthy? Or did the conflict simply lack the intensity of other civil wars that year such as Bosnia, Afghanistan, Peru, and Georgia, all of which incurred more casualties, and all of which thus received more coverage?

The previous chapter showed clear evidence of a concrete reality baseline's impact on news, as well as the relatively limited influence of governmental elites and press organizations in a political domain with a divided elite and little meaningful variance in press norms and constraints. This chapter examines foreign conflicts coverage, a domain with a unified, motivated elite, an agreed-upon but perhaps difficult-to-perceive reality baseline, and meaningful variation in press norms and constraints primarily along one dimension. Specifically, I model variation in *New York Times* coverage of all intra-state conflicts (civil wars) in the world between 1992 and 1997, transcending the contingencies of particular conflicts to produce a large-scale model of foreign conflicts coverage.

CONFLICTS COVERAGE

News coverage of conflicts, and foreign affairs in general, garners considerable scholarly attention, mostly in the form of single or small-n comparative case studies. Also, conflicts in which the United States participates directly receive most of the attention. This makes sense, given that such conflicts get the bulk of foreign policy news coverage (Gans 1979). Studies of U.S.-involved conflicts both during the Cold War (Hallin 1984, Hertog 2000) and after (Herman 1993, Bennett and Paletz 1994, Mermin 1997, Livingston and Eachus 1995, Robinson 2000) have spawned influential theoretical insights, including Bennett's "indexing" theory (1990), which has been expanded and tested under a variety of conditions (see Mermin 1999; Althaus, Edy, Entman, and Phalen 1996; Bennett, Lawrence, and Livingston 2007).

As these studies focus on a small number of cases, they provide a rich account of coverage tone and its implications for many of the most important democratic theoretical questions about the press's role in American politics. Less common, though, are models of coverage trends that are generalizeable across a large set of conflicts, both with and without United States involvement. Though several studies build models of general foreign coverage (see Van Belle 2000, Adams 1986, and Singer, Endreny, and Glassman 1991 for systematic analyses of natural disasters coverage, and Wu 2000, Chang, Shoemaker, and Brendlinger 1987, and Kariel and Rosenvall 1984 for models of foreign coverage), none of them focuses on conflicts.

Of course conflicts to which the United States is a party deserve the attention they receive in the literature, given that U.S. material, financial, and human resources are at stake. However, given that a small, remote conflict ignored by the United States can transform suddenly into famine, genocide, or trans-continental mayhem, it is important to model the news media's role in bringing some conflicts to the forefront of the public consciousness while others are left to simmer out of view.

PREDICTORS OF COVERAGE

The Correlates of War project (Sarkees and Schafer 2000) documents all wars from 1816–1997 that meet a definitional threshold. Utilizing area experts and international documentation, it is more than a mere reflection of United States news coverage, and thus serves as suitable external documentation of this study's universe. I limit the analysis to intrastate (civil) wars in the post-Cold War era, specifically 1992–1997.[1] Intrastate wars "are those between or among two or more groups *within* the internationally recognized territory of a state" in which "the central government at the time was actively involved, effective resistance. . . occurred on both sides, and at least 1,000 battle deaths resulted during the civil war" (Sarkees and Schafer 2000, 129).

The unit of analysis is a conflict during a given year (conflict-year): Bosnia in 1992, Burundi in 1994, Sudan in 1997, and so on, for a total of 108 cases.[2]

Reality Baseline: The Actual Intensity of Civil Wars

Measuring the actual, objective magnitude of a conflict presents several challenges. First, many potential indicators, such as Red Cross aid or UN involvement, have complex, intertwined relationships with other variables of interest (media coverage, presidential influence), and thus are inappropriate as measures of the exogenous "reality" of a conflict. Further, the most intuitively appealing measure, *battle deaths*, is only available for approximately three-fourths of the cases.

To take advantage of the conceptually appealing but incomplete battle-deaths variable without disregarding a quarter of the cases, I run two separate analyses. The first discards one-fourth of the cases in order to use the battle-deaths variable. This is a tally of estimated battle deaths that year (*Stockholm International Peace Research Institute Yearbook* 1992–1998), divided by 1,000 for ease of interpretation. The second uses all of the cases by taking advantage of an alternative measure of war intensity: the number of *displaced persons*. This measure is the sum of the number of refugees and internally displaced persons that year (*World Refugee Survey* 1991–1998), divided by 100,000.

Presidential Influence

Though President Clinton had inherited the United States' involvement in Somalia from his predecessor, the ultimate failure of the mission was put squarely on Clinton's shoulders in public discourse. The loss of 18 U.S. soldiers in October, 1993—an event immortalized in the movie "Black Hawk Down"—led to a rapid U.S. withdrawal from the conflict, the resignation of Secretary of Defense Les Aspin, and an increasing reluctance on the part of the government to engage in nation-building. It was less than a year, however, before the Rwandan catastrophe commanded the world's attention. Clinton, still stinging from the Somalia embarrassment, was reluctant to give in to the mounting international pressure to stem the genocide by force. He was so reluctant, in fact, that he instructed his staff not to refer to the devastation as "genocide" (Jehl 1994).

When an administration tries to avoid public pressure for intervention in a potentially difficult situation, or more generally when a president wants to make optimal foreign policy decisions free from public scrutiny (Baum 2004), are they able to keep it off the public radar screen by failing to mention it in speeches and ignoring press conference questions? Conversely, how successful are the president and his administration when they desire to publicize a particular conflict?

Scholars argue that the modern president is heavily reliant on the press for bargaining with rival policy makers, as well as for maintaining the public esteem that is crucial for the success of such bargaining (Kernell 1997, Cook 1998). The symbiotic relationship between the president and the press often is complicated by divergent views over what statements and actions are newsworthy (Cook). The presidential news beat thus takes on the character of a sophisticated game, with each side having high stakes riding on its ability to win the struggle for news definition.

I measure presidential attempts to influence the news product with a count of all *White House mentions* of a conflict during each conflict-year, found through a search of the Lexis-Nexis transcripts database. A "White House mention" is defined here as a public statement in any form by the president—including news conferences, Rose Garden remarks, national speeches, road speeches, public remarks after an event, campaign speeches and press releases—or by an official White House spokesperson in a news conference or press release.[3]

But what if White House attention itself is driven by reality? Given the clear causal precedence of reality over White House mentions, any variation shared by the variables might cause overestimation of the president's unique effect. In fact, battle deaths and White House mentions are correlated at a statistically significant .230, while displaced persons and White House mentions are correlated at a remarkable .000. Apparently, it took death, rather than mere displacement, to gain the attention of presidents Bush and Clinton. To eliminate the shared variation between battle deaths and White House mentions, I create a new "purged" White House mentions variable from the residuals of an OLS regression of White House mentions on battle deaths.[4]

Independent Media Influence over Conflicts Coverage

The final category of independent variables gauges the phenomena that drive variation in news content solely on account of their convergence with the norms, routines, and constraints of professional journalism. "Proximity," a classic news judgment criterion found in introductory journalism textbooks and countless news content studies, works as an ideal starting point from which to deduce hypotheses about conflict coverage. After all, "distance" from the United States is a key source of variability between the different conflict-afflicted countries. Studies that approach foreign affairs and disaster coverage from a systematic and comparative vantage point inform many of the measures (see Wu 2000, Van Belle 2000, Adams 1986, Singer, Endreny, and Glassman 1991, Kariel and Rosenvall 1984, Chang, Shoemaker and Brendlinger 1987, Ostgaard 1965, Hester 1973, Galtung and Ruge 1965). The variables spring from two broad types of proximity: physical and cultural.

Physical proximity of the conflict's host country to the United States might impact coverage for a number of press-organizational reasons. First, from a logistical standpoint, news organizations tend to have a greater number of permanent correspondents closer to the United States. Also, dispatching correspondents to a conflict site when necessary is easier to accomplish for Peru rather than Myanmar. The *direct distance*, in kilometers, between New York City and the country's capital serves as the measure of physical proximity (Fitzpatrick and Modlin 1986). Additionally, I calculated the distance between the country's capital and the *nearest* New York Times *correspondent*, as of 1995 (Graber 1997).

Cultural proximity is widely believed in popular discourse to be a key determinant of foreign coverage. Critics argue "10,000 deaths in Nepal equals 100 deaths in Wales equals 10 deaths in West Virginia equals one death next door"[5] (Diamond 1975). The Nepal-Wales contrast, of course, goes beyond pure physical proximity. The degree of cultural similarity to the United States—be it ethnic, religious, linguistic, economic or ideological—comports directly with several logistical and audience-related considerations for American news organizations, including their ability to report with ease from the country, and the American audience's interest in the country's affairs. Gans (1979) bluntly notes that "in foreign news. . . [o]ther countries [are judged by] the extent to which they live up to or imitate American practices and values."

As population, economic power, and "eliteness" of the war-torn country have been shown to explain disaster and foreign affairs coverage across countries (see studies cited above), it is reasonable to posit a similar effect on conflict coverage. Two forms of GNP serve as measures of a country's size. *Absolute GNP* works as a composite measure of population and economic strength, while *GNP per capita* along with the amount of *trade* (imports + exports, Department of Commerce 2002) conducted with the United States serve as measures of economic proximity/relevance to the United States.

Other aspects of cultural proximity are tricky to operationalize. Scholars often use an indicator of the country's primary language and its proximity to English (Chang, Shoemaker and Brendlinger 1987, Hester 1973, Van Belle 2000, Wu 2000). *Language translatability* is a direct measure of the ease with which a news organization is able to cover a country's affairs. Additionally, it serves as a proxy for some of the more nebulous aspects of cultural proximity, including cultural affinity and, in keeping with the concerns of critical theorists that the American press is ethnocentric, the "whiteness" of the country's population. To measure language proximity, I created a scale of a language's similarity to English, based on the linguistic concept of language families. Each country's score is a composite of the country's languages' scale value, weighted by the degree to which each language is spoken by the general population, as well as by whether it is one of the official languages of the country.[6] The appendix gives the full formula, along with the rest of the independent variable measurement schemes.

Because of high multicollinearity, the media-power indicators can only wield their true influence if distilled into composite factors representing the underlying concepts. To identify these factors, I run a principal components analysis of the six indicators (Table 5.1). The first two factors, together explaining almost seventy percent of the variance in the six indicators, will be used as independent variables. The first factor loads largely on three indicators of *economic proximity* to the United States (GNP, GNP Per Capita, and Trade). The second combines the proximity of a *New York Times* correspondent with language translatability, suggesting an underlying *media logistics* dimension, meaning the ease—both physical and cultural—with which the *Times* can cover the involved country. Preliminary analyses confirmed that these factors perform better than any single indicator of media norms and constraints. As a side note, neither factor is correlated with White House mentions; thus no further purging of the latter is necessary.

Table 5.1. **Media Power Factors**

	First Factor	*Second Factor*
NYT Correspondent	.22	.83
GNP	.76	.01
GNP Per Capita	.74	−.54
Distance	−.55	.26
Trade	.91	.05
Language	.42	.73
Eigenvalue	2.48	1.58
Percent of Variance	41.34	26.29

Note: Entries are loadings derived from a principal components analysis.

ANALYSIS

The dependent variable is a simple count of the number of *New York Times* stories in which each conflict is mentioned during each year. The peculiar nature of the data poses several methodological barriers to robust estimation. The cases are grouped by two categories, time and conflict. As such, there are 32 conflicts and 6 years, but only 108 cases. Some battles, such as Sri Lanka, Sudan, and Algeria, persist for all 6 years, while others, such as El Salvador and Mozambique, ended in 1992. Essentially, the data are of a panel structure, but with severe attrition and late entry. Further, tricky causal questions and potentially influential cases necessitate a series of remedies, each dealt with below. Fortunately, the culmination of the analyses brings several robust findings.

Table 5.2 shows the conflicts that received the most and least coverage. The four Bosnia years each produced more coverage than any other conflict year, with the least of them receiving roughly the same amount of coverage as the next three conflict-years combined. Several Somalia years also commanded disproportionate coverage. Direct United States involvement is obviously an important factor contributing to American media coverage.

Table 5.2. Twenty Conflict Years with the Most and Least Coverage

Most		Least	
Conflict (Year)	*Articles (#)*	*Conflict (Year)*	*Articles (#)*
Bosnia (1993)	1001	Burma (1995)	0
Bosnia (1994)	844	Sierra Leone (1993)	1
Bosnia (1995)	801	Rwanda (1992)	2
Bosnia (1992)	788	Pakistan (1994)	2
Russia-Chechens (1995)	280	Sierra Leone (1992)	4
Somalia (1993)	259	Sierra Leone (1994)	4
Somalia (1992)	233	Burma (1993)	5
Rwanda (1994)	209	Rwanda (1993)	5
Zaire (1997)	205	Uganda (1996)	5
Somalia (1994)	131	Zaire (1993)	6
Burundi (1996)	113	Sierra Leone (1996)	7
Zaire (1996)	102	Sri Lanka (1992)	8
Cambodia (1993)	101	Mozambique (1992)	11
Azerbaijan (1992)	89	Philippines (1992)	12
Somalia (1995)	89	Sudan (1995)	13
Russia-Chechens (1996)	86	Azerbaijan (1994)	13
Somalia (1996)	86	Burundi (1993)	13
Peru (1992)	77	Pakistan (1995)	13
Algeria (1995)	75	Uganda (1997)	13
Angola (1993)	70	Peru (1994)	14

This presents a dilemma. On the one hand, as these cases come to mind immediately when most observers think of conflicts in the 1990s, arbitrary limitation of the population to exclude them from the analysis would be theoretically problematic. However, their inclusion might give undue explanatory weight to a small proportion of the cases. So as not to make an arbitrary decision about inclusion of the U.S.-involved cases, I run two sets of models, one with and one without them. I add a *United States involvement* dummy variable to the inclusive models, signifying the four Bosnia and six Somalia cases.

Also, the dependent variable is skewed, with a mean of 75 but a range of 0 to 1001 (or, when U.S.-involved cases are excluded, a mean of 39 and a range of 0 to 280). Most conflict years received fewer than 65 articles. To minimize this skew, I transform the dependent variable, along with the similarly skewed battle deaths, displaced persons, and White House mentions variables, by taking them to their natural log. As this transformation eliminates the direct interpretability of the coefficients, I take the additional step of standardizing each variable to maximize the comparability of their magnitudes (the two media-power factors are already standardized).

Looking at the results (Table 5.3), we can dispense easily with any distinction between non-U.S.-involved wars only and the full data set. Apparently, inclusion of the heavily covered U.S.-involved conflicts does not change the relationship between the variables, as the coefficients for all relationships are nearly identical across the two renderings. Subsequent analysis thus will focus on all conflicts (the top half of Table 5.3). To interpret the magnitude of each coefficient, note that the articles variable is centered at 0 (for all cases) or .14 (for the battle-deaths-valid cases), with a standard deviation of 1 and a total range of –2.83 to 2.82.

First, U.S. involvement indeed emerges as a powerful predictor of media coverage. Also, when the White House's statements diverge from reality, they apparently carry media coverage with them. The mentions variable is significant and of a relatively large magnitude across all of the models. Less remarkable are the two media-power variables. Economic proximity has a small but consistent effect on articles, while media logistics is only significant in the second model.

The effect of actual conflict intensity depends on the measure. Just as the president apparently pays more attention to a higher magnitude of deaths but not refugees or internally displaced persons, so too does the *New York Times* give greater play to conflicts with high casualty levels. For the 73 cases for which battle-deaths data were available, every standard deviation increase in deaths brings a third of a standard deviation more coverage. On the other hand, the displaced persons variable fails to make a substantive or statistical impact.

Table 5.3. *New York Times* Coverage of Foreign Conflicts, 1992–1997

	All Conflicts			
	B	SE	B	SE
Reality				
Battle Deaths	.34*	.06		
Displaced Persons			.04	.06
Media Power				
Economic Proximity	.17*	.06	.20*	.07
Media Logistics	−.07	.06	−.15*	.07
Elite Influence				
White House Mentions	.51*	.10	.62*	.09
U.S. Involvement	.80*	.32	.59*	.29
(Constant)	.02	.07	−.06	.07
N	73		108	
Adj. R−squared	.69		.58	

	Without U.S. Involvement			
	B	SE	B	SE
Reality				
Battle Deaths	.33*	.07		
Displaced Persons			.02	.07
Media Power				
Economic Proximity	.17*	.06	.19*	.07
Media Logistics	−.07	.06	−.14*	.07
Elite Influence				
White House Mentions	.49*	.11	.61*	.10
(Constant)	.02	.08	−.06	.07
N	66		98	
Adj. R-squared	.40		.34	

Notes: OLS regression; coefficients are unstandardized, but all variables except the U.S. Involvement dummy are standardized (mean= 0, sd = 1).

* $p < .05$

Table 5.4.   Comparing All Cases to Valid Battle-Death Cases

	All Cases		Battle-Death Cases Only	
	Mean	SD	Mean	SD
Articles	0	1.00	.15	.94
White House Mentions	0	1.00	−.06	1.02
Displaced Persons	0	1.00	−.02	1.02
Economic Proximity	0	1.00	.27	1.05
Media Logistics	0	1.00	−.08	1.10
N	108		73	

Thus far, the assumption has been made that any difference in explanatory power between deaths and displaced persons arises from differences in the measures themselves. However, an alternative explanation is that the 73 battle-death-valid cases differ in a systematic way from the whole data set of 108 conflict years. We can shed some light on the question by comparing the levels of key variables between the two data sets. Table 5.4 shows the extent to which the battle-death-valid cases deviate from the standardized values in the full data set. Clearly, the differences are minimal. The battle-death cases enjoy slightly greater economic proximity to the United States, though the difference is only about a quarter of a standard deviation, or 8 percent of the entire range of the variable. They also garner slightly more articles. But no difference comes even close to a standard deviation of a variable, and it would be difficult to make a case that any of these differences are consequential for the models. Thus, I make the assumption hereafter that the differences in explanatory power between battle deaths and displaced persons is attributable to real differences between the two variables.

As noted above, the peculiar nature of the data require additional specifications to test for robustness. I now turn to the various barriers to estimation.

Reciprocity

The recursive models above rest on the assumption that White House mentions precede coverage. The temporal order between mentions and coverage is an important question substantively as well as theoretically. If the order is as hypothesized here, then the press cedes agenda-setting power to the president. If, on the other hand, the administration decides which conflicts require attention by reading the *New York Times*, then the power belongs to the press. Accordingly, the so-called "CNN effect," by which media attention to foreign situations leads to U.S. intervention, receives considerable attention in the literature. The findings are mixed, though recent literature seems to suggest that the presumed causal order in this study is reasonable. Mermin (1997) studied the interaction between the press and the government regarding Somalia, finding that "journalists ultimately made the decision to cover Somalia, but the stage for this decision had been set in Washington." Livingston and Eachus (1995) and Robinson (2000) also found that elites led the Somalia coverage, while the latter found that the media helped set the stage for the Bosnia intervention.

The true causal sequence is nearly impossible to estimate empirically from these data. Though a non-recursive system of simultaneous equations would be ideal, the lack of potential instrumental variables precludes this solution for the present data. Also, as the data are not of a strictly time-serial nature, Granger Causality tests are impossible to perform on the whole data set. Nonetheless, I took advantage of the time element to create Granger Causality tests for the two most heavily covered conflicts: Bosnia and Somalia. First, I disaggregated each to month. I then predicted coverage from its own first two lags, with the next model adding the first two lags of mentions. A block F-test shows whether the mentions lags added any explanatory power. This was repeated with mentions as the dependent variable. Of course, this does not directly address the question of causality in the cross-sectional data; but it at least will be suggestive of the interplay between the president and the press in two high-profile conflicts, while adding a new methodological twist to the CNN-effect literature.

The results are mixed (Table 5.5). On the one hand, Bosnia provides strong evidence to support the presumed direction of causality in this analysis. The effect of White House mentions on coverage is significant at the .05 level, whereas coverage in no way improves the prediction of mentions. On the other hand, the causal flow for Somalia is bidirectional, with each block F-test similarly significant and the improvement of prediction roughly equivalent for

Table 5.5.   Granger Causality Tests, Bosnia and Somalia by Month

	Bosnia	Somalia
News Coverage Granger-Causes Presidential Mentions	.11	4.21*
Presidential Mentions Granger-Causes News Coverage	5.04*	3.43*
N	192	205

Notes: *p<.05. Values reported are block F-tests with (2,188) degrees of freedom for Bosnia, and (2,201) for Somalia. Analysis is bivariate Vector Autoregression using four separate OLS regression models: one reduced model for each of the two dependent variables and two full models. Each full model includes two lags of the dependent variable and two lags of the predictor variable. Each reduced model eliminates the lags of the predictor variable. Block F-tests determine whether the block of two lags of the predictor variable improves the model fit.

each direction. This test, while providing some evidence to support the presumed direction, shows that the true story is complicated. Ultimately, within the scope of this analysis, I choose to rely on the plausible and literature-bolstered assumption that White House mentions drive coverage.[7]

Panel Data?

The peculiar structure of the cases as unwieldy panel data raises additional concerns. Specifically, to the extent that the errors are correlated between cases within a given conflict—and that extent is tremendous—the potential exists for overconfident standard error predictions. With only 73 cases, any solution will eat away at critical degrees of freedom, and therefore will be a tough test of the previous findings.

I account for correlated errors with two additional estimations of the battle-deaths model, each employing highly conservative assumptions. First, coverage is predicted by reality and White House mentions, with the effect of each conflict fixed by the inclusion of 22 dummy variables for (n-1) conflicts (Table 5.6). This essentially examines only the effect of each predictor across time. Unfortunately, the economic proximity and media logistics variables do not vary over time, and thus are not estimable in this model. Interestingly, while the White House mentions variable drops out, the battle-deaths variable retains its statistical significance, even with the brutal restrictions on this model. This is a powerful indicator of that variable's robustness.

Next, I washed out the effect of time by aggregating the data to conflict, rather than conflict year. The unit of analysis becomes the average yearly value over the duration of the conflict. In this new data set of 23 cases (Table 5.7), both the White House mentions and battle-deaths variables show a statistically significant and substantively powerful effect, while economic prox-

Table 5.6. Explaining Coverage with Fixed Conflict Effects

	B	SE
Battle Deaths	.21*	.07
White House Mentions	.11	.16
(Constant)	.14	.18
N	73	
Adj. R-squared	.78	

Notes: OLS regression; coefficients are unstandardized. 22 conflict dummy variables included in the model were excluded from this presentation.
* p<.05

Table 5.7.   **Explaining Coverage, Aggregated to Conflict**

	B	SE
Battle Deaths	.60*	.09
Economic Proximity	.20*	.09
Media Logistics	-.06	.10
White House Mentions	.64*	.14
U.S. Involvement	.45	.43
(Constant)	.05	.09
N	23	
Adj. R-squared	.80	

Note: OLS regression; coefficients are unstandardized.
* p<.05

imity retains its significance. Overall, the model is robust, even in the face of conservative restrictions.

DISCUSSION

In the foreign conflicts domain, the general reluctance of Congress to criticize the president, as well as the asymmetric power constitutionally allotted and effectively exercised by the president, cause elites to speak with a relatively unified voice. The fruit born of this unity manifests itself in the president's ability to set the press agenda for foreign conflicts, consistent with the elite consensus hypothesis.

The president and especially the press, however, were largely constrained— presumably on account of credibility concerns—by the actual magnitude of the conflict during the period of analysis. Despite being difficult, and some- times dangerous, for journalists to perceive, "reality" is a powerful predictor of variation in coverage. American journalists appear to be skilled—to a heretofore-unappreciated degree—at holding a mirror to the domain of foreign conflicts, despite the rhetorical contestation inherent in warfare. Interestingly, displaced persons fails as a proxy measure of battle intensity, as both the pres- ident and the press appear to spring to attention only in the presence of death. On the other hand, the differences between conflicts in their physical and cul- tural proximity to the United States apparently shape the routines, and thus the output, of *New York Times* reporters and editors only weakly.

While this chapter and the prior one illustrate how a concrete reality can limit media influence, the next chapter showcases the full force of the news media's potential to act as a powerful, independent political institution.

APPENDIX

Dependent Variable

The dependent variable is a count of the number of *New York Times* stories in which each conflict is mentioned during each year. A "mention" is any reference, in any context, to the ongoing civil war in that country. A query was created for Lexis-Nexis that brought about all stories in a year that mentioned the affected country for each of the 108 conflict years ["(country name)" in full text. For Georgia, "not Atlanta" was used to minimize irrelevant articles]. Tens of thousands of stories were found. Each story was then read in its entirety by one of three coders, two of whom were blind to the nature and hypotheses of the project. After the coders were trained, they coded identical samples of 100 coding choices along several objective and subjective dimensions. The only code choices used in the present study involved this simple question: Did this article mention the conflict? The three coders agreed unanimously on these choices. Stories were eligible for coding if they were in the front section or the financial section, and were not capsules of stories that appeared elsewhere.

Raw Components of the Independent Variables

Refugees (mean = .57, sd = 2.20, min/max = 0/16.48)—Change in the number of refugees (in hundreds of thousands) from the previous year. Negative values reverted to zero. (*World Refugee Survey*)

Internally Displaced (mean = 1.41, sd = 2.89, min/max = 0/15)—Change in the number of internally displaced citizens (in hundreds of thousands) from the previous year. Negative values reverted to zero. (*World Refugee Survey*)

Displaced Persons (mean = 1.98, sd = 4.01, min/max = 0/23.40) –Refugees plus internally displaced (each as calculated above).

Battle Deaths (mean = 3.37, sd = 5.06, min/max = 0/25.00)—Estimated number of battle deaths (in thousands) that year. (*Stockholm International Peace Research Institute Yearbook*, 1992–1998)

NYT Correspondent (mean = 2087.77, sd = 1294.66, min/max = 0/4112)—Direct distance (as the crow flies) in kilometers between the capital of the country and a city with the nearest *New York Times* correspondent, as of 1995. (Graber 1997)

GNP (mean = 59.62, sd = 113.93, min/max = .70/427.40)—Gross National Product in billions of U.S. dollars, most recent estimate as reported in the 2001 *Europa World Yearbook*.

GNP Per Capita (mean = 877.46, sd = 916.64, min/max = 110/3160)—Gross National Product per capita in U.S. dollars, most recent estimate as reported in the 2001 *Europa World Yearbook*.

Distance (mean = 9808.92, sd = 2923.97, min/max = 3339/14218)—Direct distance (as the crow flies) in kilometers between the capital of the country and New York City.

Trade (mean = 2023.00, sd = 3064.29, min/max = 8/12302)—Millions of dollars of trade (imports + exports) between the country and the United States. (Department of Commerce Website)

Language (mean = 1.95, sd = .60, min/max = 1/3)—a scale that is a function of which languages are spoken in the country and how prominently, and proximity of the language to English. A proximity score, ranging from 1 to 5, was assigned to each language according to the following scheme:

5: English. 4: Other Germanic. 3: Celtic or Romantic. 2: Other Indo-European. 1: Non-Indo-European

For countries in which only one language was listed in the *Europa World Yearbook*, the proximity score is used as the value for this variable. For countries with multiple languages, the various languages were weighted according to their prominence within the country. If the languages were listed in *Europa* according to the percentage of citizens who speak them, then those percentages are used as the weights. If the languages were listed qualitatively, then the following coding scheme was used, which is exhaustive of the various manners in which the languages were categorized:

(1) "Official" 50%. "Others widely spoken" 50%.
(2) "Official" 35%. "Associate official" 25% "Others widely spoken" 40%.
(3) "Official" 50%. "Others widely spoken" 25%. "Spoken by substantial minority" 25%.

White House Mentions (mean = 9.37, sd = 30.46, min/max = 0/203)—A count of the number of times the conflict is mentioned by the president in any public capacity, or by an official White House spokesperson in a news conference or press release. (Original content analysis, Lexis-Nexis Political Transcripts database)

U.S. Involvement—A dummy variable for the six Somalia and four Bosnia cases.

Note: Descriptive statistics are for unstandardized, unlogged versions of variables.

NOTES

1. The period of analysis begins in 1992 to keep it within a post–Cold War alignment. The Correlates of War data set ends in 1997. A vast majority of the conflicts in this era were civil wars, so I limited it to that universe to minimize poten-

tial confounding factors. For example, the many country-specific variables would not be applicable to a war with more than one participant.

2. Iraq vs. the Kurds is excluded from the analysis because of the impossibility of disentangling its coverage from that of the recently completed Gulf War.

3. Though it would also be interesting to examine Congress's ability to set the foreign policy agenda, such data were difficult to gather with this study's combination of broad scope and limited resources.

4. It might be argued that a correlation of .23 is not enough to bring about a collinearity threat. Nonetheless, given the indisputable causal precedence of reality over White House mentions, the best estimate of their unique effects within a single regression analysis can be obtained with a purged mentions variable.

5. A variation of this adage is "One dead fireman in Brooklyn is worth five English bobbies, who are worth 50 Arabs, who are worth 500 Africans" (Boyer 1985, cf. Singer, Endreny, and Glassman 1991).

6. One complication to this formulation would be if the separatist faction spoke a language that was different, with respect to its proximity to English, than the host country (Quebec declaring war on Canada, for example). Fortunately, no such situation appears to exist in this data set.

7. If in fact the relationship were reciprocal, this would manifest itself in two ways. First, the estimated coefficient for the effect of White House mentions would be exaggerated. To the extent that the reader fails to buy my assumption about the causal order, this should be taken into account. Next, to the degree that the White House mentions variable was correlated with the other independent variables, the coefficients for such variables might be underestimated. Fortunately this was not a problem; the purged White House mentions variable is not correlated with any of the other predictors.

Chapter Six

Supreme Court News

"I keep hearing about the decision with the Supreme Court with the homosexual ruling. I just want to say I think it's a beautiful thing. Because if you really think about it, you know, the more gay men there are in the world, that just leaves more chicks for me and you, Wolf."—Musician Kid Rock, on CNN's Wolf Blitzer Reports, June 17, 2003.

Not all Supreme Court decisions are sexy enough to be mentioned by an eccentric pop star during a fluff cable interview. Accordingly, Court and communication scholars surely would not be surprised that Kid Rock neglected to mention a case concerning arbitration of contract-related disputes, decided three days prior to the heavily covered *Lawrence v. Texas*. Nor would they be surprised that the entire national press corps ignored it. It is intuitively obvious that *Lawrence* possessed more news appeal than a dry contract-law case. "Dry" is not synonymous with "inconsequential," however; nor does "sexiness" reveal anything about a case's importance to legal precedent, the concerned parties, or the public.

This chapter models the factors that explain the likelihood of a Supreme Court case from the 2002 term receiving attention in the national print and broadcast media. Given that cases vary wildly in their potential appeal to a news audience—from abortion, affirmative action, and Internet porn to obscure jurisdictional disputes—the classic news judgment criteria of color, timeliness, simplicity, and so on, are clearly "invoked" in this domain. The prediction that flows directly from the invocation of constraints hypothesis, therefore, is that a case's fit with the classic news judgment criteria will explain considerable variation in case coverage. This chapter, then, showcases a domain in which maximal independent media influence is expected.

NEWS COVERAGE OF THE SUPREME COURT

Why do some Supreme Court decisions receive more coverage than others in national print and broadcast sources? This analysis models the factors that affect the likelihood of a decision from the Supreme Court's 2002 term being mentioned in the *New York Times*, on CNN, and on the three network evening news programs.

The Effect of Issue Area

Slotnick and Segal's (1998) in-depth examination of the Supreme Court's treatment by television news included a model explaining coverage variation during the 1989 term. As indicated by the title of that chapter—"Which Decisions are Reported? It's the Issue, Stupid!"—they found the issue area of the case to be among the strongest predictors of coverage. First Amendment and criminal justice cases were far more likely to be covered by network television than other issue areas. This gave rigorous, multivariate corroboration to previous studies with similar findings across different media and time periods (Solimine 1980, Tarpley 1984, Bowles and Bromley 1992, O'Callaghan and Dukes 1992). More recently, Maltzman and Wahlbeck (2003) analyzed front-page *New York Times* coverage of Supreme Court decisions from 1953-1990. Among the many significant predictors, they found that cases dealing with First Amendment and Civil Liberties issues received more coverage, on average, than other issue areas.

In addition to introducing multivariate analysis to the mix, Slotnick and Segal improved upon the previous studies' methods of categorizing issue areas. O'-Callaghan and Dukes (1992), for example, collapsed the *National Law Journal's* issue classifications into five categories: civil rights, criminal law, economic issues, First Amendment, and other. However, Slotnick and Segal argue that, "our own work has convinced us that the *Journal's* classifications are frequently based on an inaccurate identification of the fundamental legal conflict in the cases" (215). They also argue that the five issue areas are too limiting and often shoehorn diverse cases into the same heading. To remedy these shortcomings, they created a broader array of issue areas—First Amendment, criminal justice, other rights and liberties, judicial power, federalism, economic, and other. Also, to label the cases more accurately, they categorized them after "a full reading of each case's syllabus reported in the *U.S. Reports*" (219).

Classic News Judgment Criteria

As with the prior studies, Slotnick and Segal's rationale for the effect of issue area was the power of "the commercial dictates of television news and concerns about audience appeal, interesting visuals, conflict, and drama" in the selection of newsworthy cases from the universe of decisions during a given year (219). In the language of the present framework, this is independent media influence: a non-spurious effect of the norms and constraints of professional journalism—in this case the classic news judgment criteria of color, drama, timeliness, simplicity, and so forth—on variation in news content.

While the strengths of Slotnick and Segal's analysis are considerable, they rely ultimately on a blunt, indirect measure of a case's fit with news judgment criteria (NJC hereafter). While the inference that First Amendment cases fit better on average with the classic NJC than federalism cases is entirely reasonable, it is an inference nonetheless. To give the notions of color, drama, and simplicity a fair chance to exert their full effect over news coverage, however, it would be ideal to measure them at the individual case level, as every other variable is measured. After all, even Slotnick and Segal's more nuanced categories compress a considerable amount of meaningful variance into the NJC. For example, in the 2002 term, the cases that would fit into the criminal justice category include *Ewing v. California* and *Lockyer v. Andrade*, which dealt with the hot-button, heavily covered three-strikes laws, and *Woodford v. Garceau*, which addressed the dryer, more complicated issue of the timing of habeas applications with the enactment of a federal death penalty statute. The latter case received no coverage in any national outlet.

Measuring a case's fit with the NJC presents a formidable challenge. No existing indicator comes anywhere close to tapping the "color" or "simplicity" of an individual case; nor do the building blocks for such a measure make themselves apparent in any archive or public record. To overcome these obstacles, I construct a measure by going straight to the source: journalists. Specifically, three professional reporters coded summaries of the 78 decisions with opinions from the 2002 term along five different dimensions that were intended to tap a case's fit with the NJC. The coders were political reporters (none from a law/court/judicial beat) from two major metropolitan newspapers. Two of the reporters are located in the Southwest, and the other works in his paper's Washington bureau. The coding took place in early 2006.

The coders were offered a nominal fee to read summaries of each of the 78 cases, as printed in the American Bar Association's annual *Preview of United States Supreme Court Cases* publication (2003). The ABA summaries are ideal because they are relatively short (one or two meaty sentences) and do a good job of capturing the substantive and legal issues that court reporters would evaluate for newsworthiness. The reporters were not shown the case names, and any American state mentioned in the summary was changed to a similarly sized state in a different region. Also, their instruction sheet referred to the project only as the "News and Courts Study," and they were told that the cases were "real and hypothetical Supreme Court cases." They were also instructed not to consult any outside resources, so that the coding would tap merely "your opinion." At no time were they given even a hint that the purpose was to measure news judgment.

They were asked to evaluate each summary along five dimensions, each of which was described in one sentence with which they were asked to "strongly disagree," "disagree," "neutral," "agree," or "strongly agree." The five sentences were:

(1) The general public would perceive this case as interesting.
(2) If covered by the press, the case has the potential to arouse intense emotional reactions from sizeable segments of the public.
(3) The issues involved in the case are simple enough for the public to understand.
(4) The case involves one or more hot contemporary public policy issues.
(5) The issues involved in the case personally affect sizeable segments of the American public.

The first two, hereafter known as *interesting* and *emotional*, tap concepts related to the notions of color and drama. The third taps simplicity (*simple* hereafter), the fourth measures how *timely* the involved issues are, and the fifth is an indicator of *impact* on the news audience.

Fortunately, despite the subjective nature of the task, the coders agreed with each other to an acceptably high degree for the first four concepts. The Cronbach's alpha scores for the variables were as follows: interesting = .87, emotional = .82, simple = .77, timely = .80, and impact = .57. Impact is excluded from the analysis hereafter. Each of the four acceptable indicators was turned into an additive scale, divided by 3 to make it a 1-5 metric. The four scales were too highly correlated with each other to be included as predictors in the same regression analysis, but not so similar that they failed to wield divergent impacts on the dependent variable. Thus, separate models are estimated with each NJC variable.

OTHER PREDICTORS: INDEPENDENT VS. SPURIOUS MEDIA INFLUENCE

The conceptual framework divided the determinants of news content into three different categories: reality, elites, and independent media influence. First, the realities underlying the relative importance of Supreme Court cases are soft at best. There are no external, universally agreed-upon criteria for evaluating the importance of a decision. Still, Maltzman and Wahlbeck (2003) note that cases vary in the degree to which they represent "major legal change," such as finding a law unconstitutional or altering precedent. Such change might be construed as a quasi-reality baseline, in that it represents the case's concrete impact on the law, irrespective of the interest it might generate among elites or the public. For 2002, Spaeth's (2006) Original U.S. Supreme Court Judicial Database from the S. Sidney Ulmer Project contains measures of whether the case altered precedent and whether it struck down a law as unconstitutional. Unfortunately, only one case altered precedent in the 2002 term—the high-profile *Lawrence v. Texas* sodomy law case. On the other hand, five cases overturned laws. The dummy variable *unconstitutional* flags these cases. The *New York Times*, in catering to a relatively sophisticated audience with more in-depth stories, is expected to show the largest effect for this variable.

Elite Influence: In the Supreme Court domain, several sets of elite actors hold a stake in the Court's decisions. The most obvious are the justices themselves. Unlike other political actors, however, the justices take no direct action to garner or spin news coverage. Their only press-management tactic, therefore, is the decisions they write. As Maltzman and Wahlbeck (2003) note,

> Separate opinions are one sign of division among justices and are frequently written as a vehicle for garnering press attention and public notice (Davis 1994, 115–116). . . Since news from the Supreme Court relies on justices' written opinions, rather than interviews (Davis 1994), opinions are the only expression of reasons for disagreement with the majority opinion (7).

Following Maltzman and Wahlbeck, I calculate the number of *separate opinions* (dissenting or concurring) written for each case using Spaeth's (2006) data. Past studies have also used a measure of the case vote or the size of the majority coalition. For 2002, however, such an indicator is too highly correlated with the separate opinions measure to warrant inclusion in the model.

The presidential administration also has a stake in publicizing or criticizing some Supreme Court decisions. Unlike the justices, however, administrations attempt to set the press's agenda on a daily basis. The federal government's involvement in Supreme Court cases varies greatly. At one extreme, the United States was a direct party to thirteen cases during the 2002 term. This is measured with a *U.S. Direct Involvement* dummy variable. Also, a representative of the government made an oral argument in 51 cases and filed an *amicus* brief in 47 of them. As those cases have almost perfect overlap, only the *U.S. Oral Argument* dummy variable is used.

As much as the government cares about certain case outcomes, no actor expends more time and energy attempting to influence press coverage of the Supreme Court than interest groups. The elite salience hypothesis thus predicts that interest groups should have more impact on the press's agenda than the president or even the justices.[1] As representatives of subgroups within the citizenry, interest groups might be said to represent popular, rather than elite, influence. However, given the biases in interest group formation, maintenance, and effectiveness, it is at best an elite-leaning public for whom they speak (Schlozman and Tierney 1986, Salisbury 1984, though see Lowery and Gray 2004). The clearest measure of the degree of interest among pressure groups is the total number of *amicus briefs* filed for a case. Following Slotnick and Segal's (1998) effort to minimize the skew in this indicator, I "measured the number of briefs filed in a case by intervals of five, with zero indicating no briefs, 1 indicating up to five briefs filed, 2 indicating up to ten briefs, and so on. If there were more than twenty-five briefs filed in a case, it was coded as 6" (219).

Media Power: The NJC variables serve as the most direct measures yet of independent media power over the decision to cover a Supreme Court case. Though they are expected to wield influence over all media, it is reasonable to hypothesize that they might have a larger impact over television news than its more thorough and sophisticated print counterpart (especially the one known as the "Gray Lady").

In addition to the NJC, other press-organizational factors might affect variation in decision coverage. First, Slotnick and Segal (1998) found that cases received less coverage, on average, on days in which more decisions were announced. After all, a 22-minute newscast can only hold a limited amount of information. For this multiple-outlet study, organizations with the smallest news hole (network evening news) should be more likely than the others (CNN, *New York Times*) to exclude cases that might otherwise warrant coverage on a slower Supreme Court *decision day*.

Finally, under the rationale of the official sources bias, Maltzman and Wahlbeck (2003, 8) find that opinions authored by the chief justice are more likely to be covered than others. From Spaeth's (2006) data, I use a dummy variable indicating Chief Justice *Rehnquist's* authorship of the opinion. This is arguably a hybrid indicator of media and elite influence, as it is essentially the influence of one particular elite, on account of a press quirk. It thus should be viewed as a control variable only.

Dependent Variables: News Coverage of 2002 Decisions

Each dependent variable is a dummy variable indicating whether the case was mentioned in any capacity in the outlet, from the moment the decision was announced to one week after the decision. For network evening news, the variable measures whether a decision is mentioned on at least one of the three networks (CBS, NBC, ABC). The complete content of the outlets' news output was searched using the Lexis-Nexis Major Papers Database (*New York Times*) and News Transcripts Database (television) from November 4, 2002, to July 3, 2003.

ANALYSIS

What percentage of Supreme Court cases do various media outlets bother to cover? Table 6.1 shows how many of the 78 decisions with opinions in the 2002 term garnered mentions in the national press. Not surprisingly, network evening news shows covered the fewest number of decisions. CBS, the network with the most illustrious news tradition, covered 15. All told, just over 20 percent of the cases were mentioned on any network, and only six mustered the attention of all three.[2] Meanwhile, CNN bested the combined networks slightly by covering just under a quarter of the decisions. On the other hand, the *New York Times* covered exactly half of the cases, putting 14 of them on the front page, and featuring decision excerpts from seven.

Logit analysis for each of the three outlets shows which factors affect the likelihood of a decision receiving at least one mention. For each outlet, a different model is estimated for each of the four News Judgment Criteria variables. For ease of interpretation, the odds ratios appear in brackets under the unstandardized coefficients.

Table 6.1. Coverage of 2002 Supreme Court Decisions, within One Week after Decision

Outlet	# of Decisions Covered	Percent of Total Decisions
ABC	9	11.5
CBS	15	19.2
NBC	8	10.3
At Least One Network	17	21.8
At Least Two Networks	9	11.5
All Three Networks	6	7.7
CNN	19	24.4
CNN, multiple days	6	7.7
New York Times	39	50.0
New York Times, front page	14	17.9
New York Times, case excerpt	7	9.0

Note: Total decisions (with opinions) during term = 78

Table 6.2. Predicting CNN coverage of 2002 Supreme Court Decisions

	CNN			
	(1)	*(2)*	*(3)*	*(4)*
U.S. Direct Involvement	−1.95 (1.50)	−1.73 (1.54)	−2.01 (1.45)	−1.82 (1.57)
	[.14]	[.18]	[.14]	[.16]
U.S. Oral Argument	.18 (.79)	.18 (.80)	.29 (.77)	.39 (.83)
	[1.20]	[1.20]	[1.33]	[1.48]
Amicus Briefs	.73 (.31)*	.75 (.32)*	.79 (.33)*	.79 (.32)*
	[2.07]	[2.12]	[2.20]	[2.20]
Separate Opinions	.01 (.28)	−.08 (.30)	.18 (.27)	−.24 (.32)
	[1.01]	[.93]	[1.20]	[.79]
Unconstitutional	.98 (1.33)	.84 (1.42)	1.08 (1.25)	1.74 (1.46)
	[2.65]	[2.31]	[2.95]	[5.71]
Rehnquist	1.14 (1.05)	1.28 (1.04)	1.01 (.96)	1.33 (1.17)
	[3.13]	[3.61]	[2.75]	[3.78]
Decisions/Day	−.24 (.25)	−.20 (.26)	−.16 (.24)	−.17 (.26)
	[.79]	[.82]	[.85]	[.84]
Interesting	.98 (.41)*			
	[2.66]			
Emotional		1.19 (.45)*		
		[3.29]		
Simple			.63 (.44)	
			[1.87]	
Timely				1.51 (.54)*
				[4.51]
(Constant)	−5.14 (1.52)	−5.79 (1.69)	−4.51 (1.56)	−7.04 (2.09)
N	78	78	78	78

Notes: Logit analysis, coefficients are unstandardized.
Cells: B (S.E.)
[Odds Ratio]
*p<.05

Tables 6.2, 6.3, and 6.4 present logit models for CNN, the networks, and the *Times*, respectively. First, to understand the magnitude of the NJC variables' impact, note that they are averaged five-point scales (strongly disagree to strongly agree). Their descriptive statistics (mean, standard deviation) are similar: interesting (3.08, 1.16), emotional (2.95, 1.10), simple (3.11, 0.93), and timely (2.97, 1.12). Thus, a one-point change is always roughly a one-standard-deviation change, while a three-point change encompasses 80 to 90 percent of the cases, depending on the variable. An odds ratio of more than one is interpreted as "for every one-point increase in the independent variable, a case was, on average, [odds ratio] times as likely to be covered than a case with a one-point lower score on the independent variable, other factors

Table 6.3. Predicting Network Evening News Coverage of 2002 Supreme Court Decisions

	Network Evening News			
	(1)	(2)	(3)	(4)
U.S. Direct Involvement	1.12 (1.24)	1.42 (1.21)	.57 (1.10)	1.51 (1.27)
	[3.07]	[4.12]	[1.78]	[4.54]
U.S. Oral Argument	.43 (.99)	.42 (1.01)	.59 (.95)	.72 (1.02)
	[1.54]	[1.52]	[1.81]	[2.05]
Amicus Briefs	−.04 (.39)	.03 (.40)	.03 (.38)	.03 (.45)
	[.95]	[1.03]	[1.03]	[1.03]
Separate Opinions	.33 (.35)	.25 (.36)	.57 (.33)+	.03 (.40)
	[1.39]	[1.29]	[1.76]	[1.03]
Unconstitutional	3.87 (1.68)*	3.84 (1.76)*	3.80 (1.58)*	5.41 (2.14)*
	[47.79]	[46.59]	[44.88]	[223.38]
Rehnquist	.43 (1.14)	.87 (1.10)	.41 (1.05)	.66 (1.26)
	[1.54]	[2.38]	[1.51]	[1.93]
Decisions/Day	−.23 (.31)	−.16 (.30)	−.20 (.29)	−.09 (.32)
	[.80]	[.85]	[.82]	[.91]
Interesting	1.76 (.64)*			
	[5.82]			
Emotional		1.89 (.72)*		
		[6.63]		
Simple			1.46 (.61)*	
			[4.32]	
Timely				2.41 (.91)*
				[11.08]
(Constant)	−8.28 (2.54)	−8.72 (2.78)	−7.60 (2.38)	−10.89 (3.57)
N	78	78	78	78

Notes: Logit analysis, coefficients are unstandardized.
Cells: B (S.E.)
[Odds Ratio]
*p<.05

held constant." An odds ratio between 0 and 1 indicates a negative relationship, in which a one-point increase in the independent variable makes a case "[odds ratio x 100] percent as likely to be covered. . ."

True to the invocation of constraints hypothesis, the NJC were by far the most consistent predictors—in fact, they were the only factors that influenced coverage for all three outlets. As expected, network news is most structured by the NJC. For every additional simplicity point, a case was more than four times as likely to be covered—and that was the least powerful NJC variable. For every additional timeliness point, a case was 11 times as likely to be covered. Interestingly, there was no clear difference between CNN and the *Times* in propensity to use the NJC. The largest impact for CNN was timeliness, with a

4.5 odds ratio, and simplicity did not even attain statistical significance. Likewise, the *Times* odds ratios range from 3 to just over 4.

The elite influence variables also performed as hypothesized. The number of *amicus* briefs influenced CNN and the *Times*, while U.S. involvement and the number of separate opinions failed to influence any outlet. Every additional point on the 0-6 briefs measure (mean = 1.42, standard deviation = 1.33) yielded a case of twice as much coverage on CNN and two and a half times as much in the *Times*.

On the other hand, the results for the decisions-per-day variable contradict the predicted relationships. Despite having a larger news hole than the networks, the *Times* was the only outlet sensitive to the number of decisions announced that day. The relationship is strong: a decision that shares a day with

Table 6.4. Predicting *New York Times* coverage of 2002 Supreme Court decisions

	New York Times			
	(1)	*(2)*	*(3)*	*(4)*
U.S. Direct Involvement	.72 (.98)	.49 (.89)	.63 (.96)	.39 (.87)
	[2.06]	[1.64]	[1.87]	[1.48]
U.S. Oral Argument	1.07 (.81)	1.00 (.80)	.81 (.76)	1.16 (.79)
	[2.91]	[2.73]	[2.25]	[3.20]
Amicus Briefs	.88 (.40)*	.89 (.40)*	1.13 (.41)*	.93 (.39)*
	[2.40]	[2.43]	[3.10]	[2.53]
Separate Opinions	.36 (.36)	.44 (.37)	.53 (.36)	.43 (.36)
	[1.43]	[1.56]	[1.69]	[1.53]
Unconstitutional	.88 (1.55)	.79 (1.54)	1.13 (1.52)	1.24 (1.49)
	[2.42]	[2.20]	[3.11]	[3.45]
Rehnquist	−1.08 (1.55)	−.91 (1.39)	−1.55 (1.43)	−1.08 (1.42)
	[.34]	[.40]	[.21]	[.34]
Decisions/Day	−.57 (.25)*	−.50 (.24)*	−.51 (.24)*	−.42 (.22)
	[.57]	[.61]	[.60]	[.66]
Interesting	1.47 (.45)*			
	[4.36]			
Emotional		1.46 (.47)*		
		[4.32]		
Simple			1.33 (.44)*	
			[3.76]	
Timely				1.11 (.39)*
				[3.05]
(Constant)	−4.89 (1.50)	−4.95 (1.52)	−5.00 (1.51)	−4.41 (1.41)
N	78	78	78	78

Notes: Logit analysis, coefficients are unstandardized.
Cells: B (S.E.)
[Odds Ratio]
*p<.05

one other decision is only 60 percent as likely to be covered as one that was announced alone (when controlling for the other factors), and so on. Perhaps the *Times*'s more thorough coverage actually enables this relationship. That is, in covering fully half of all decisions, many cases from the excluded half might be falling through the cracks on busy decision days. On the other hand, television outlets cover so few decisions, awaiting strong cues such as fit with the NJC, that the danger of wanting to cover more than one case in a day is minimal.

The most peculiar finding is network news's privileging of decisions that render laws unconstitutional. The partial effect is monstrous: such a case is around 45 times as likely to be covered as a case that does not overturn a law (with one discrepant model putting the odds ratio considerably higher). Most likely, this is a fluke generated by the skewed nature of the unconstitutional variable, in that only five cases overturned laws. Network news covered four of those five cases (80 percent), so the partial effects were bound to be formidable. It is unclear, however, why network news would give so much weight to that criterion, if they indeed did so.

DISCUSSION

The theory of conditional media influence predicted that the Supreme Court domain would be highly susceptible to the classic news judgment criteria of color, drama, simplicity, and so forth. As characteristics of the domain vary tremendously along those dimensions, journalists would incur a high cost by straying from such criteria. Sure enough, when measured at the unique case level, the NJC are a powerful, robust predictor of which cases received coverage in the 2002 term. In fact, they are the only powerful, robust predictor. As with many political domains, then, the dynamics of the Supreme Court/public opinion nexus cannot be understood without careful attention to the quirks of American press organizations.

APPENDIX

Dependent Variables

Dependent variables are dummy variables indicating whether the case was mentioned in any capacity on CNN (mean = .24, sd = .43, min/max = 0/1), in the *New York Times* (mean = .50, sd = .50, min/max = 0/1), or on one of the three networks (mean = .22, sd = .42, min/max = 0/1), from the moment the decision was announced to one week after the decision. The one-week limit prevents a bias toward cases early in the term that garnered residual mentions in later articles. Because of the one-week limit, end-of-term wrapups were excluded to avoid privileging cases decided during the last week of the term.

The complete content of the outlets' news output was searched using the Lexis-Nexis Major Papers Database (*New York Times*) and News Transcripts Database (television) from November 4, 2002, to July 3, 2003. For each outlet, the full text was searched for the term "Supreme Court." Each story found was read in its entirety to determine whether it mentioned a decision from no more than one week prior. This broad, exhaustive search assured that no stories were overlooked. *New York Times* editorial/opinion content was excluded. Also, a case must have been mentioned in the text of an article, not just in a graphic or chart.

Independent Variables
News Judgment Criteria (NJC) Variables

The NJC variables are averages of the scores (1–5) given by the three expert coders as to a case's relative fit with each NJC, as detailed in the text. Four of the five variables attained a satisfactory level of intercoder reliability to be included in the full analysis: interesting (mean = 3.08, sd = 1.16, min/max = 1.33/5.00), emotional (mean = 2.95, sd = 1.10, min/max = 1.33/5.00), simple (mean = 3.11, sd = .93, min/max = 1.33/5.00), and timely (mean = 2.97, sd = 1.12, min/max = 1.00/5.00).

Steps were taken at all phases of the project to minimize the risk that these variables would be considered tautological—in other words, too close conceptually to the dependent variable such that they are tapping the effect of news selection on itself, rather than modeling a distinct causal relationship. Several steps were mentioned in the text: using local reporters, avoiding the court beat, not revealing the nature of the study, and changing state names in the summaries. Also, the year of the cases was chosen carefully to balance the need for "timeliness" to be meaningful and the need for a temporal buffer to minimize the prospect of the coders remembering a case from its actual media coverage. Though three years would seem like enough time to minimize the prospect of contamination, I tested for it empirically by rerunning the logit analyses with the three most high-profile cases eliminated—the Michigan affirmative action cases, the Texas sodomy law case, and the three-strikes cases. By any reasonable estimate, these are the only cases that a non-court reporter would remember from three years prior. The results, available upon request from the author, differ in no meaningful way from the results of the full models.

Other Independent Variables

Unconstitutional (mean = .06, sd = .25, min/max = 0/1)—A dummy variable indicating whether the case overturned a law. From the Original U.S. Supreme Court Judicial Database from the S. Sidney Ulmer Project.

Separate Opinions (mean = 1.33, sd = 1.40, min/max = 0/6)—The number of dissenting or concurring opinions issued for the case.

U.S. Direct Involvement (mean = .17, sd = .38, min/max = 0/1)—A dummy variable indicating whether the U.S. government was a direct party to the case.

U.S. Oral Argument (mean = .65, sd = .48, min/max = 0/1)—A dummy variable indicating whether a representative of the U.S. government made an oral argument in the case.

Amicus Briefs (mean = 1.42, sd = 1.33, min/max = 0/6)—The total number of amicus briefs filed for the case. 0 = no briefs; 1 = 1-5 briefs; 2 = 6-10 briefs; 3 = 11-15 briefs; 4 = 16-20 briefs; 5 = 21-25 briefs; 6 = more than 25 briefs.

Decisions/Day (mean = 3.28, sd = 1.50, min/max = 1/6)—The number of decisions handed down by the Supreme Court on the day of the case's decision.

Rehnquist (mean = .14, sd = .35, min/max = 0/1)—A dummy variable indicating Chief Justice William Rehnquist's authorship of the opinion.

NOTES

1. Were this a study of coverage tone, the elite consensus hypothesis would predict the opposite outcome—that the ideological split among interest groups would render their influence negligible. However, as I am only examining the setting of the press's agenda, interest groups are united on all sides in their desire to see the decisions covered.

2. The six decisions featured on all three networks dealt with the University of Michigan's affirmative action program, the Family and Medical Leave Act, library access to Internet pornography, state sodomy laws, abortion protests, and state "three strikes" laws.

Chapter Seven

Conclusion

The study of American politics stands to benefit from doing two things: recognizing the press as a powerful political institution, and understanding the conditions and limitations of this power. This book has argued that the key to understanding the conditional influence of the press in politics lies in accounting for the factors that shape the political news product. The influence that news content wields over public opinion, electoral politics, policy output, or discourse—commonly known as media effects—cannot accurately be attributed to the media, as a political institution with a unique contribution to discourse and outcomes, if one of two conditions exists: (1) variation in such coverage follows an agreed-upon and readily observable reality baseline, rendering the press a mere information carrier, or (2) elites successfully shape the news content, rendering journalists mere lapdogs rather than watchdogs. On the other hand, such influence rightly belongs to the press to the extent that the political phenomena that sway coverage do so on account of either the professional norms that define journalism as a distinct form of mass communication, or the financial mandate to produce as low-cost a product as possible with maximum audience appeal. Thus, a necessary but overlooked step in understanding the nature and extent of the press's role in any given political domain is to model systematic variation in news coverage thereof, with an eye toward the three categories of news influence.

The theory of conditional media influence spells out the conditions under which the press is more or less an independent political actor in a given domain, and, conversely, when they cede their power to other actors or phenomena. The theory derives from the tension between the three categories of news influence put forth in the conceptual framework.

First, in politics—a realm of semantic and practical contestation if there ever was one—not all "realities" are equally real. Elite discourse, policy output, and public opinion sometimes are bounded by external facts that limit the universe of plausibility for a given action or statement—and there is no reason to believe that credibility-conscious journalists should be any different. But sometimes no such constraint exists in the nature of the domain. The more agreed upon and readily observable realities exist in a domain, the more news content will flow with them, and thus the less news organizations will wield meaningful influence.

Next, elite expenditures of time and resources to shape the news are more successful when elites are in consensus rather than conflict, and when the issue warrants priority status among the many phenomena competing for their limited time and resources.

Finally, any one of the myriad normative and financial constraints that drive the journalism profession can influence a political domain, but only if the constraint is "invoked," meaning that potentially newsworthy elements of the domain vary in the extent to which they accord with the constraint. The greater the number of constraints invoked in a domain, the more news is shaped with respect to the constraints, and thus the more independent influence the press wields in the domain.

The empirical chapters explored the character and extent of media influence in politics by modeling systematic variations in news content in three different substantive political arenas, each with high interest in popular discourse and scholarly inquiry. In addition to their self-contained appeal as explorations of three important political arenas, they act in tandem as a first test of the theory of conditional media influence.

The strong impact of reality on economic coverage, especially the more concrete "conditions" coverage, was expected. Reality's considerable impact on foreign conflicts coverage, however, was more novel. Neither systematic studies of foreign news flow nor studies of individual foreign conflicts give credit to the constraining power of a reality baseline. But in this first large-scale study of foreign conflicts, reality emerged as a formidable constraint on both elite rhetoric and news content.

While the economic and conflict domains are not necessarily representative of the most common issue areas covered by political journalists, these findings should serve nonetheless as a caution not to ignore the potential of external reality to shape the behavior of news organizations and to moderate the impact of news content on the various political processes it has been shown to affect. Though few realms are as comprehensively governed by a concrete reality as economics, relatively few are entirely free from potentially constraining aspects of reality either.

For example, the failure of the Monica Lewinsky affair to dent President Clinton's approval rating puzzled observers of all political stripes. This domain would seem to be a marquee example of an intractable battle over the construction of reality—was it about high crimes, misdemeanors, and obstruction of justice? Or was it a petty political persecution stemming from a small sexual fib? But embedded in the rhetoric are elements of agreed-upon reality. For example, no serious, disinterested party would conclude that Clinton's crimes were comparable to those of Watergate. Whether one believes that Clinton's crimes exceeded the impeachment threshold ultimately was an intractable matter of partisan taste; but I would argue that the Watergate-Lewinsky variation in "reality" acted as an important baseline. Though the press's passivity (see chapter 2) might have rendered it unable to present the case in those terms, this variation in reality likely did not escape notice by attentive citizens. Much is known about factors that limit the media's sway over public opinion. The accordance of the message with reality needs to be taken seriously, and given further scrutiny in future research, as another potential media-effects moderator.

To what degree did the press set its own agenda through its norms and constraints? Accordant with the invocation of constraints hypothesis, the realm in which constraints were most meaningfully invoked—the Supreme Court—brought forth a considerable impact. The Supreme Court study was thus a strong indicator of the importance of taking the press seriously as an independent player in many of the most important political processes. In foreign conflicts coverage, however, physical and cultural proximity bore only modest explanatory fruit, despite the argument that closer conflicts are both easier to cover and more appealing to a news audience. Perhaps the tremendous attenuation of media influence from the combination of reality and elites left little variation to be explained. Or perhaps, given the advances in communications and travel technology, as well as the United States' complex role in the multi-polar, post–Cold War world, the variation in the constraints between covering Colombia and Zaire might not be as meaningful as suspected.

Whatever the case, the foreign conflicts chapter highlights the importance of not tacitly attributing all variation in the political news product to the independent, unattenuated actions of news organizations. By making such a case, this project endeavors to contribute an important insight across a wide swath of modern political science: the news media are an endogenous political institution, deserving of the same nuanced empirical treatment of other linkage institutions such as parties and interest groups. Though the rich literature on media effects has contributed much to our knowledge of public opinion and policy output, its typical treatment of news content as exogenous precludes the press from receiving full consideration in mainstream empirical explorations of mass-elite linkage and inter-institutional relations.

IRAQ WAR REVISITED

In the first chapter, I noted that diverse observations about news coverage of the U.S. invasion of Iraq could be reconciled by the book's theoretical framework. Though the earlier discussion focused on accusations of bias, the fully specified framework lends insight into other aspects of the war coverage as well, including its presumed effect on public opinion.

In February 2007 the AP/Ipsos poll tested respondents' knowledge of American and Iraqi deaths in the Iraq War (Benac 2007). Assuming that citizens' knowledge of events in Iraq comes mostly from the press, the results aptly showcase the difference between the press's influence under a concrete reality and under conditions in which press norms and elite preferences have more room to wield power.

First, the poll suggests that citizens hear a consistent story regarding American deaths. The median guess among respondents was that there had been 2,974 American military personnel killed, reasonably close to the actual figure of 3,154 as of the poll's dates. Fully 61 percent of respondents guessed between 2000–4000.

On the other hand, the guesses as to the number of Iraqi civilian deaths were unreliable and too low. The website Iraq Body Count compiles Iraqi civilian deaths that have been reported in at least two credible news sources, thereby making it an extremely conservative estimate of actual casualties. As of the week of the AP/Ipsos poll, its estimate was 57,000 to 63,000. At the higher end, a controversial 2006 study published in the British medical journal the *Lancet* placed the midpoint of the statistical estimate at 655,000 total Iraqi deaths attributable to the war (Burnham, et. al. 2006). Even President Bush acknowledged in December 2005 that approximately 30,000 civilians had been killed, a number that matched the Iraq Body Count estimate of the time (Dorell 2005).

How close were the respondents to even the most unrealistically conservative estimates? The median guess was 9,890, with almost a quarter of respondents guessing 1000–5000. Only 22 percent guessed more than 50,000, with half of those (11 percent of total) saying more than 100,000.

What explains the discrepancy in citizen accuracy? First, the number of American battle deaths is as concrete a reality as possible in news coverage of warfare. The government keeps an official, detailed tally, readily accessible to news organizations. Even if presidential administration officials desired to downplay the number of deaths, an intentional undercount simply would not be feasible. After all, the families of the fallen would promptly notice any omissions. The media, having no choice but to report this agreed-upon and easily perceivable reality, do so faithfully. Though the frequency with which they report the body count is a matter of editorial judgment, it is a reasonable assumption that viewers demand frequent updates on this ubiquitous barometer of a war's progress.

On the other hand, it is extremely difficult to count Iraqi deaths. Custom dictates that bodies be buried immediately, and many bodies go completely under official radar, sometimes never even making it to a morgue. Also, the United States government—on which domestic news sources are heavily dependent—chose not to make Iraqi body counts a priority, to put it mildly. Additionally, the line between soldier and civilian tends to be blurrier in the age of suicide bombers. To overcome these problems, the *Lancet* researchers literally risked their lives to go door-to-door in the cluster-sampled neighborhoods, some of which were in the most dangerous areas in the country. Even so, their confidence intervals are wide, and even some war opponents criticized their 2006 finding.[1] Thus the number of American deaths, as a more agreed-upon and easily observed reality than Iraqi deaths, was transmitted in a manner that apparently facilitated a higher degree of accurate perception by news consumers.

Beyond the relative concreteness of the two realities, other factors described in the framework likely were at play as well. For example, much to the chagrin of internationalist scholars and critics, the news judgment criterion of "proximity" is invoked to a tremendous degree in this domain. The American news audience cares far more about the number of American deaths than those of Iraqi soldiers or civilians. As a result, the American death tally appeared at least once or twice a week in every major news outlet. On the other hand, though the death estimates from each day's bombings tended to be aired, mentions of cumulative Iraqi casualty counts were scarce, notwithstanding the coverage received by each of the two *Lancet* studies.

THE FUTURE: NEWS, PUBLIC OPINION, AND THE INTERNET

The early twenty-first century is a perilous time for keepers of the old political communication order. Newspaper circulation continues to decline rapidly, as each paper struggles with the trade-off between trying to save the old business model and navigating the uncertain and fast-changing world of Internet-based content and revenue generation. Fox News Channel has reintroduced the notion of ideologically branded news to the mainstream media world, to great success. In ever-increasing competition with an ever-increasing array of distractions, local television and cable news continue their slide down the path of "soft news" (though see Baum, 2003, for an analysis suggesting that this might not be as bad for democracy as many critics argue). And of course, the Internet continues to develop as a key facilitator of political communication of all stripes.

Much of the Internet-based news comes from the websites of brick-and-mortar media outlets such as CNN and the *New York Times*. Though the web brings unique opportunities such as live streaming video, chats with reporters, and reporter blogs, there is no reason to think that this change in delivery mode will fundamentally alter the enduring norms and routines of news organizations. On the other hand, weblogs ("blogs") hold the potential to transform political communication in fundamental ways.

The universe of political weblogs—the "blogosphere," as it is commonly known—is a vastly diverse, unwieldy entity. Though this diversity enables its critics—usually journalists with a material interest in the status quo—to dismiss its potential by highlighting its negative aspects, a careful examination of the most popular blogs shows an emerging medium bursting with transformative potential. In particular, the new media may create, or at least enhance, a third attenuating factor to the theory of conditional media influence: the public.

Though public opinion has always played a role in setting the news agenda, the character of its influence is hardly satisfying from a democratic-theoretical perspective. As audience-calibrated revenue generation dictates the success or failure of a news outlet, the most important news judgment criteria revolve around journalists's perceptions of what the news audience wants—color, drama, timeliness, novelty, and so on. Hamilton (2004), for example, gives a detailed demonstration of the mainstream press's underappreciated ability to tailor its content to the demographics and interests of its markets. However, consultant-driven perceptions of "what the public wants" should never be confused with democratic accountability. After all, they are just perceptions. It is far from clear that the violence and celebrity obsession of television news even constitutes what a public, presented with a full, accessible array of news choices, would choose. That "chicken and egg" question—do the news media give us what we want, or do they tell us what we want?—cannot be resolved here (see McChesney 2004, ch. 5, for a compelling argument, and Rosenstiel et. al. 2007 for empirical evidence that, in fact, they do *not* give us what we want). Also, even if journalists could flawlessly perceive the fully informed desires of their audience, it would be no indicator of the democratic implications of the news-public relationship. Perhaps the most profound potential impact of the new media, then, is their ability to give citizens a more immediate and effectual role in setting the news agenda.

Bloggers and their reader-participants have many goals, ranging from mere expression and audience building to grassroots political organizing and fundraising. In the present political communication environment, still dominated by the traditional press, one of the blogosphere's key goals is to influence the content of mainstream news outlets. This is accomplished through so-called "blogswarms," in which the readers of blogs on one side of the political spectrum are whipped into a frenzy by an event—usually an "outrageous" statement or action by someone in a position of power or influence—that they perceive to be worthy of sustained news coverage. The swarm manifests first in intense discussion of the event on the most heavily trafficked blogs, and then in a deluge of e-mails and phone calls to editors and reporters at all levels by the bloggers and their reader-participants.

Do blogswarms work? The evidence is mixed. The blogosphere's high-profile successes are well known: conservative bloggers brought Dan Rather's illustrious CBS career to a premature end during the 2004 presidential election by exposing his use of forged documents allegedly showing gaps in George W. Bush's Texas Air National Guard service. Likewise, liberal blogs publicized racially insensitive comments by Senate Majority Leader Trent Lott, eventually forcing his temporary ouster from Senate leadership.

On the other hand, the big victories—setting the press's agenda on fundamental questions of public policy—appear elusive. In another study (Schiffer 2006b), I examined the effectiveness of one such blogswarm, the 2005 liberal frenzy over the Downing Street Memos. The memos, leaked to and printed in the *Times of London* in May of 2005, are the minutes of a top-secret meeting between British Prime Minister Tony Blair and top intelligence officials from July of 2002. They contain several quotes that were seen by liberal activists as the "smoking gun" proving that the Bush administration knowingly misled the nation into war. Among the most cited was the report of the head of British Intelligence, after a trip to the United States, that "Bush wanted to remove Saddam, through military action, justified by the conjunction of terrorism and [weapons of mass destruction]. But the intelligence and the facts were being fixed around the policy." No single incident had excited the liberal blogosphere to the degree that the memos did, yet the story was ignored at first by the mainstream press. The intense swarm that followed over the next two months thus provided a test of their power over the news agenda. Though the persistent publicity by blogs, and the thousands of letters to media outlets that it generated, helped produce a brief burst of mainstream coverage in June of 2005, a high proportion of the straight news coverage was pegged to President Bush's only comment on the issue. The official sources bias thus trumped the blogswarm on television and on the news pages of major American newspapers. However, the activists were apparently more successful at generating a sustained level of newspaper editorials, opinion columns, and printed letters to the editor in major newspapers.

Time will tell whether blogswarms become a regular part of the news agenda-setting process, or whether professional journalists become accustomed to the new noise level and tune them out, just as they were accustomed to a steady stream of letters to the editor. Even if their influence does increase, blogs would represent a narrow, stylized form of democracy. For obvious reasons, the blog audience tends to be far more politically aware and active than average citizens. Still, even if journalists have no reliable barometer of general public sentiment, the attentive public whose voice is suddenly amplified by blogs represents at least a step toward the democratization of political communication.

NOTE

1. The Iraq Body Count website—with ostensibly the same goal as the *Lancet* researchers—is nonetheless full of criticism of their study.

References

Adams, William C. "Whose Lives Count?: TV Coverage of Natural Disasters." *Journal of Communication* 36, no. 2 (Spring 1986): 113–22.

Althaus, Scott L., Jill A. Edy, Robert M. Entman, and Patricia Phalen. "Revising the Indexing Hypothesis: Officials, Media, and the Libya Crisis." *Political Communication* 13, no. 4 (October-December 1996): 407–21.

Baker, Brent, and Rich Noyes. 2003. "Grading TV's War News." *Media Research Center*. <http://www.mrc.org/specialreports/2003/sum/execwarnews.asp>

Baum, Matthew A. *Soft News Goes to War: Public Opinion and American Foreign Policy in the New Media Age*. Princeton, N.J.: Princeton University Press, 2003.

——. "How Public Opinion Constrains the Use of Force: The Case of Operation Restore Hope. *Presidential Studies Quarterly* 34, no. 2 (June 2004): 187–226.

Behr, Roy L., and Shanto Iyengar. "Television News, Real-World Cues, and Changes in the Public Agenda." *Public Opinion Quarterly* 49, no. 2 (Summer 1985): 38–57.

Benac, Nancy. "Americans Underestimate Iraqi Death Toll." *Associated Press*, 24 February, 2007.

Bennett, W. Lance. *News: The Politics of Illusion. 6th ed*. New York: Longman, 2005.

——. "Toward a Theory of Press-State Relations in the U.S." *Journal of Communication* 40, no. 2 (Spring 1990): 103–25.

Bennett, W. Lance., and David L. Paletz (eds.). *Taken by Storm: The Media, Public Opinion, and U.S. Foreign Policy in the Gulf War*. Chicago: University of Chicago Press, 1994.

Bennett, W. Lance, Regina G. Lawrence, and Steven Livingston. *When the Press Fails: Political Power and the News Media from Iraq to Katrina*. Chicago: University of Chicago Press, 2007.

Berkowitz, Dan. "TV News Sources and News Channels: A Study in Agenda-Building," *Journalism Quarterly* 64, no. 2 (Summer-Autumn 1987): 508–13.

Bowles, Dorothy A., and Rebekah V. Bromley. "Newsmagazine Coverage of the Supreme Court During the Reagan Administration." *Journalism Quarterly* 69, no. 4 (Winter 1992): 948–59.

Boyer, Peter. "Famine in Ethiopia." *Washington Journalism Review* 7 (January 1985): 18–21.

Brody, Richard A. *Assessing the President: The Media, Elite Opinion, and Public Support.* Stanford, Calif.: Stanford University Press, 1991.

Brown, Jane Delano, Carl R. Bybee, Stanley T. Wearden, and Dulcie Murdock Straughan. "Invisible Power: Newspaper News Sources and the Limits of Diversity." *Journalism Quarterly* 64, no. 1 (Spring 1987): 45–54.

Burnham, Gilbert, Riyadh Lafta, Shannon Doocy, Les Roberts. "Mortality after the 2003 Invasion of Iraq: A Cross-Sectional Cluster Sample Survey." *The Lancet* 368, no. 9545 (21 October 2006): 1421–28.

Chang, Tsan-Kuo, Pamela J. Shoemaker, and Nancy Brendlinger. "Determinants of International News Coverage in the U.S. Media." *Communication Research* 14, no. 4 (August 1987): 396–414.

Cook, Timothy E. *Governing with the News: The News Media as a Political Institution.* Chicago: University of Chicago Press, 1998.

Cunningham, Brent. "Re-thinking Objectivity." *Columbia Journalism Review* 42, Issue 2 (July/August 2003): 24–32.

Davis, Richard. *Decisions and Images: The Supreme Court and the Press.* Englewood Cliffs, N.J.: Prentice Hall, 1994.

De Boef, Suzanna, and Paul M. Kellstedt. "The Political (and Economic) Origins of Consumer Confidence." *American Journal of Political Science* 48, no. 4 (October 2004): 633–49.

Department of Commerce Trade Data. <http://www.ita.doc.gov/td/industry/otea/us-fth/tabcon.html trade data> (3 Jul. 2002).

Diamond, Edwin. *The Tin Kazoo: Television, Politics, and the News.* Cambridge, Mass.: MIT Press, 1975.

Dixon, Travis L., and Daniel Linz. "Overrepresentation and Underrepresentation of African Americans and Latinos as Lawbreakers on Television News." *Journal of Communication* 50, no. 2 (Spring 2000): 131–54.

Dorell, Oren. "Bush Puts Death of Iraqis at 30,000." *USA Today* (online) <http://www.usatoday.com/news/washington/2005-12-12-bush-iraq_x.htm> (12 Dec. 2005).

Eaton, Sabrina. "Kerry Preaches Jobs and Values in Western Ohio." *Plain Dealer*, 2 August 2004, 6(A).

Entman, Robert M. *Projections of Power: Framing News, Public Opinion, and U.S. Foreign Policy.* Chicago: University of Chicago Press, 2004.

Epstein, Edward Jay. *News from Nowhere: Television and the News.* New York: Random House, 1973.

Erikson, Robert S., Michael B. MacKuen, and James A. Stimson. *The Macro Polity.* Cambridge: Cambridge University Press, 2002.

Europa World Yearbook, 42nd Ed. London: Europa Publications Limited, 2001.

Farsetta, Diane, and Daniel Price. "Fake TV News: Widespread and Undisclosed." Center for Media and Democracy, April 6, 2006. <http://www.prwatch.org/fakenews/execsummary>

Fitzpatrick, Gary L., and Marilyn J. Modlin. *Direct Line Distances: International Edition.* Scarecrow Press: Metuchen, N.J., 1986.

Fogarty, Brian J. "Determining Economic News Coverage." *International Journal of Public Opinion Research* 17, no. 2 (2005): 149–72.

Galtung, Johan, and Mari Holmboe Ruge. "The Structure of Foreign News." *Journal of Peace Research* 2, no. 1 (1965): 64–91.

Gans, Herbert. *Deciding What's News: A Study of CBS Evening News, NBC Nightly News, Newsweek and Time.* New York: Pantheon Books, 1979.

Goldberg, Bernard. *Bias: A CBS insider exposes how the media distort the news.* Washington, D.C.: Regnery Publishing, 2002.

Graber, Doris A. *Mass Media and American Politics,* 5th ed. Washington: Congressional Quarterly Press, 1997.

Hallin, Daniel C. "The Media, the War in Vietnam, and Political Support: A Critique of the Thesis of an Oppositional Media." *Journal of Politics* 46, no. 1 (February 1984): 2–24.

Hamilton, James T. *All the News That's Fit To Sell: How the Market Transforms Information into News.* Princeton, N.J.: Princeton University Press, 2004.

Harrington, David E. "Economic News on Television: The Determinants of Coverage." *Public Opinion Quarterly* 53, no. 1 (Spring 1989): 17–40.

Herman, Edward S. "The Media's Role in U.S. Foreign Policy." *Journal of International Affairs* 47, no. 1 (Summer 1993): 23–45.

Hertog, James K. "Elite Press Coverage of the 1986 U.S.-Libya Conflict: A Case Study of Tactical and Strategic Critique." *Journalism and Mass Communication Quarterly* 77, no. 3 (Autumn 2000): 612–27.

Hester, Al. "Theoretical Considerations in Predicting Volume and Direction in International Information Flow." *Gazette* 19, no. 4 (1973): 239–47.

Hetherington, Marc J. "The Media's Role in Forming Voters' National Economic Evaluations in 1992." *American Journal of Political Science* 40, no. 2 (May 1996): 372–95.

Holmes, Steven A. "U.S. Census Finds First Income Rise in Past Six Years." *New York Times,* 27 September 1996, 1(A).

Howell, Deborah. "A Few New Year's Resolutions." *Washington Post,* 1 January 2006, 6(B).

Iraq Body Count. < http://www.iraqbodycount.org> (25 Feb. 2007).

Iyengar, Shanto. *Is Anyone Responsible? How Television Frames Political Issues.* Chicago: University of Chicago Press, 1991.

Jehl, Douglas. "Officials Told to Avoid Calling Rwanda Killings 'Genocide.'" *New York Times,* 10 June 1994, 8(A).

Kariel, Herbert G., and Lynn A. Rosenvall. "Factors Influencing International News Flow." *Journalism Quarterly* 61, no. 3 (Autumn 1984): 509–16.

Kernell, Samuel. *Going Public: New Strategies of Presidential Leadership.* Washington, D.C.: Congressional Quarterly, 1997.

Kingdon, John W. *Agendas, Alternatives, and Public Policies.* Boston: Little Brown, 1984.

Kovach, Bill, and Tom Rosenstiel. *The Elements of Journalism: What Newspeople Should Know and the Public Should Expect.* New York: Three Rivers Press, 2001.

Kuklinski, James H., and Lee Sigelman. "When Objectivity Is Not Objective: Network Television News Coverage of U.S. Senators and the 'Paradox of Objectivity.'" *The Journal of Politics* 54, no. 3 (August 1992): 810–33.

Lazarsfeld, Paul F., Bernard Berelson, and Hazel Gaudet. *The People's Choice. 2nd Ed.* New York: Columbia University Press, 1948.

Leighley, Jan E. *Mass Media and Politics: A Social Science Perspective.* Boston: Houghton Mifflin, 2004.

Lewis, Anthony. "Abroad at Home; End of the Road." *New York Times*, 18 October 1996, 37(A).

Lippmann, Walter. *Public Opinion.* New York: Free Press Paperbacks, 1997.

Livingston, Steven, and Todd Eachus. "Humanitarian Crises and U.S. Foreign Policy: Somalia and the CNN Effect Reconsidered." *Political Communication* 12, no. 4 (Winter 1995): 413–29.

Livingston Survey. *Federal Reserve Bank of Philadelphia.* <http://www.phil.frb.org/econ/liv/index.html> (24 Jan. 2003).

Lohr, Steve. "Executives Expect Many '91 Layoffs to be Permanent." *New York Times*, 16 December 1991, 1(A).

Lowery, David, and Virginia Gray. "Bias in the Heavenly Chorus: Interests in Society and Before Government." *Journal of Theoretical Politics* 16, no. 1 (January 2004): 5–29.

Lowry, Dennis T., Tarn Ching, Josephine Nio, and Dennis W. Leitner. "Setting the Public Fear Agenda: A Longitudinal Analysis of Network TV Crime Reporting, Public Perceptions of Crime, and FBI Crime Statistics." *Journal of Communication* 53, no. 1 (March 2003): 61–73.

Maltzman, Forrest, and Paul J. Wahlbeck. "Salience or Politics: *New York Times* Coverage of the Supreme Court." Paper presented at the 2003 annual meeting of the Midwest Political Science Association, Chicago.

McChesney, Robert W. *The Problem of the Media: U.S. Communication Politics in the Twenty-First Century.* New York: Monthly Review Press, 2004.

Mermin, Jonathan. *Debating War and Peace: Media Coverage of U.S. Intervention in the Post-Vietnam Era.* Princeton University Press: Princeton, N.J., 1999.

——. "Television News and American Intervention in Somalia: The Myth of a Media-Driven Foreign Policy." *Political Science Quarterly* 112, no. 3 (Autumn 1997): 385–403.

Mutz, Diana C. "Mass Media and the Depoliticization of Personal Experience." *American Journal of Political Science* 36, no. 2 (May 1992): 483–508.

Nadeau, Richard, Richard G. Niemi, David P. Fan, and Timothy Amato. "Elite Economic Forecasts, Economic News, Mass Economic Judgments, and Presidential Approval." *Journal of Politics* 61, no. 1 (February 1999): 109–35.

Nasar, Sylvia. "World's Appetite for U.S. Products Is Still Increasing." *New York Times*, 11 November 1991, 1(A).

Niven, David. *Tilt? The Search for Media Bias.* Westport, Conn.: Praeger, 2002.

——. "An Economic Theory of Political Journalism." *Journalism and Mass Communication Quarterly* 82, no. 2 (Summer 2005): 247–63.

O'Callaghan, Jerome, and James O. Dukes. "Media Coverage of the Supreme Court's Caseload." *Journalism Quarterly* 69, no. 1 (Spring 1992): 195–203.

Ostgaard, Einar. "Factors Influencing the Flow of News." *Journal of Peace Research* 2, no. 1 (1965): 39–63.

Patterson, Thomas E. *Out of Order*. New York: Vintage Books, 1994.

Perlez, Jane. "Famous Ape, Tourist Lure, Is Shot Dead." *New York Times*, 29 May 1992, 9(A).

Preview of United States Supreme Court Cases. *American Bar Association*, Division for Public Education, 2003.

Rendall, Steve, and Tara Broughel. "Amplifying Officials, Squelching Dissent." *Fairness & Accuracy In Reporting*. <http://www.fair.org/index.php?page=1145> (15 Sep. 2003).

Robinson, Piers. "The News Media and Intervention: Triggering the Use of Air Power During Humanitarian Crises." *European Journal of Communication* 15, no. 3 (September 2000): 405–14.

Rosenstiel, Tom, Marion Just, Todd Belt, Atiba Pertilla, Walter Dean, and Dante Chinni. *We Interrupt This Newscast: How to Improve Local News and Win Ratings, Too*. Cambridge: Cambridge University Press, 2007.

Salisbury, Robert. "Interest Representation: The Dominance of Institutions." *American Political Science Review* 81, no. 1 (March 1984): 64–76.

Sarkees, Meredith Reid, and Phil Schafer. "The Correlates of War Data on War: An Update to 1997." *Conflict Management and Peace Science* 18, no. 1 (2000): 123–44.

Schiffer, Adam J. "Assessing Partisan Bias in Political News: The Case(s) of Local Senate Election Coverage." *Political Communication* 23, no. 1 (January-March 2006a): 23–39.

———. "Blogswarms and Press Norms: News Coverage of the Downing Street Memo Controversy." *Journalism and Mass Communication Quarterly* 83, no. 3 (Autumn 2006b): 494–510.

Schlozman, Kay Lehman, and John T. Tierney. *Organized Interests and American Democracy*. New York: Harper and Row, 1986.

Schudson, Michael (2002). "The News Media as Political Institutions." *Annual Review of Political Science* 5: 249–69.

Sherman, Arloc. "Income Inequality Hits Record Levels, New CBO Data Show." Center for Budget and Policy Priorities, December 14, 2007. <http://www.cbpp.org/12-14-07inc.pdf>

Shoemaker, Pamela J., and Stephen D. Reese. *Mediating the Message: Theories of Influences on Mass Media Content, 2nd Ed*. White Plains, N.Y.: Longman, 1996.

Sigal, Leon V. *Reporters and Officials: The Organization and Politics of Newsmaking*. Lexington, MA: D. C. Heath, 1973.

Singer, Eleanor, Phyllis Endreny, and Marc B. Glassman. "Media Coverage of Disasters: Effect of Geographic Location." *Journalism Quarterly* 68, no. 1/2 (Spring/Summer 1991): 48–58.

Slotnick, Elliot E., and Jennifer A. Segal. *Television News and the Supreme Court: All the News That's Fit To Air?* Cambridge: Cambridge University Press, 1998.

Solimine, Michael E. "Newsmagazine Coverage of the Supreme Court." *Journalism Quarterly* 57, no. 4 (Winter 1980): 661–3.

Soloski, John. "Sources and Channels of Local News," *Journalism Quarterly* 66, no. 4 (Winter 1989): 864–870.

Soroka, Stuart, N. "Good News and Bad News: Asymmetric Responses to Economic Information." *Journal of Politics* 68, no. 2 (May 2006): 372–85.

Spaeth, Harold J. "The Original U.S. Supreme Court Judicial Database." *The S. Sidney Ulmer Project: U.S. Supreme Court Databases.* <http://www.as.uky.edu/polisci/ulmerproject/sctdata.htm> (11 Jul. 2006).

Sparrow, Bartholomew H. *Uncertain Guardians: The News Media as a Political Institution.* Baltimore: The Johns Hopkins University Press, 1999.

Stockholm International Peace Research Institute Yearbook. Oxford: Oxford University Press, 1992–1998.

Tarpley, J. Douglas. "American Newsmagazine Coverage of the Supreme Court, 1978–1981." *Journalism Quarterly* 61, no. 4 (Winter 1984): 801–04.

Tuchman, Gaye. *Making News: A Study in the Construction of Reality.* New York: Free Press, 1978.

Van Belle, Douglas A. "*New York Times* and Network TV News Coverage of Foreign Disasters: The Significance of the Insignificant Variables." *Journalism and Mass Communication Quarterly* 77, no. 1 (Spring 2000): 50–70.

Wolf Blitzer Reports. *CNN.* 17 June, 2003. Transcript from Lexis-Nexis Academic Universe (accessed 1 July, 2006).

World Refugee Survey. Immigration and Refugee Services of America, 1991–1998.

Wu, H. Denis. "Systemic Determinants of International News Coverage: A Comparison of 38 Countries." *Journal of Communication* 50, no. 2 (Spring 2000): 110–30.

Index

About the Author

Adam J. Schiffer is an assistant professor of political science at Texas Christian University. He earned his Ph.D. at the University of North Carolina at Chapel Hill in 2003. His work focuses on the intersection of the news media and politics, with recent interests in the myth of ideological bias, the effect of the objectivity norm on news and audiences, and the potential of blogs as a new form of political journalism. His work has appeared in outlets such as *Political Behavior, Political Communication, Journalism and Mass Communication Quarterly*, and the *International Journal of Press/Politics*. He lives in Fort Worth with his wife Becky and nearly a dozen pets.